JAMESTOWN EDUCATION

# Timed Readings Plus *in Literature*

25 Two-Part Lessons
with Questions for
Building Reading Speed and Comprehension

### BOOK 1

D1029395

Mc Graw Hill **Glencoe**

JAMESTOWN EDUCATION

**Image Credits:**
**Cover** (clock) CORBIS, (book and glasses) Brand X/Jupiter Images,
(quill) CORBIS.

The *McGraw·Hill* Companies

# Macmillan/McGraw-Hill
# Glencoe

Send all inquiries to:
McGraw-Hill Companies
130 E. Randolph Street, Suite 400
Chicago, IL. 60601

ISBN: 978-0-07-879446-9
MHID: 0-07-879446-3

Printed in the United States of America.

3 4 5 6 7 8 9 10  ROV  11

# CONTENTS

# TO THE STUDENT

The purpose of this book is to help you increase your reading rate and help you better understand what you read. The 25 two-part lessons in this book will also give you practice in reading literature passages and help you prepare for tests in which you must read and interpret passages within a certain time limit.

## Reading Faster and Better

### Why Read Faster?

The quick and simple answer is that faster readers are better readers. Does this statement surprise you? You might think that fast readers miss things, causing their understanding to suffer. This is not true, for two reasons:

**1. Faster readers comprehend faster.** When you read faster, the author's message comes to you faster. The text makes sense sooner because the ideas connect sooner. The more quickly you can see how the ideas, characters, and events are related to one another, the more quickly you can understand the meaning of what you are reading.

**2. Faster readers concentrate better.** Concentration is essential for comprehension. If your mind is wandering, you won't understand what you are reading. A lack of concentration causes you to reread, sometimes over and over, in order to understand the material. Faster readers concentrate better because

there's less time for distractions to interfere with their understanding.

Here are some strategies you can use when you read the passages in each lesson.

### Previewing

Previewing before you read is a very important step. This helps you to get an idea of what a passage is about and to recall any previous knowledge you have about the subject. Here are the steps to follow when previewing.

**Read the title.** Titles are designed not only to announce the subject but also to make the reader think. Ask yourself questions, such as, Is the title about a person, a place, or an event? What thoughts does the title bring to mind? What do I already know about this subject? Also read the author's name, and ask yourself, Have I heard this author's name before? Have I ever read anything written by this author?

**Read the first sentence or two.** The first sentence can give you clues about the topic of the passage. Is the author describing the setting of the story? Is the author trying to convey a certain emotion? Is the author explaining an event or action?

**Skim the entire selection.** Glance through the selection quickly for information that will help you read fluently and with understanding.

For example, do you see any characters' names? How many characters are there? Does the passage include names of places or specific dates? This information will help you better comprehend the characters, plot, and setting as you read.

**Look at the paragraph structure.** Glance over the paragraph breaks and punctuation in the passage. Look for quotation marks and paragraph breaks that signal dialogue to determine whether the passage includes a conversation between characters. If the passage includes a conversation, you know that you will need to pay attention to what the characters say to get clues about what they are thinking and feeling.

## Reading for Meaning

The author of a work of literature is not trying to teach the reader or present factual information. Rather, the author is trying to please the reader. The author wants to share feelings and experiences with the reader, to reach him or her in a personal way. This is why the language of literature is rich with meaning.

As you practice reading literature, you develop your ability to use the information in the text to connect to the deeper meanings that the author is trying to communicate. These same skills can also be put to work when you are reading textbooks, to help you organize facts into a meaningful body of knowledge.

Here are some ways to make more sense of what you read.

**Build your concentration.** You cannot understand what you read if you are not concentrating. When you discover that your thoughts are straying, correct the situation right away. Try to avoid distractions and distracting situations. Keep in mind the information you learned from previewing. This will help focus your attention on what you are reading.

**Read in thought groups.** Try to see meaningful combinations of words—phrases, clauses, or sentences. If you look at only one word at a time (word-by-word reading), both your comprehension and your reading speed suffer.

**Ask yourself questions.** To sustain the pace you have set for yourself and to maintain a high level of concentration and comprehension, ask yourself questions as you read, such as, What does this action show about the character? or, What emotion do I feel as I read the author's description of this event?

# Mastering Reading Comprehension

## Part A

Reading fast is not useful if you don't remember or understand what you have read. The 10 questions in Part A provide two ways for you to check how well you understand the text.

## Recalling Facts

These five multiple-choice questions provide a quick way to check how well you recall important information from the passage. As you learn to apply the reading strategies described earlier, you should be able to answer these questions more successfully.

## Understanding Ideas

These five questions require you to think about the main ideas in the passage. Some main ideas are stated in the passage; others are not. To answer some of the questions, you need to draw conclusions about what you read.

## Part B

The five activities in Part B require multiple answers. These exercises provide practice in applying comprehension and critical thinking skills that you can use in all your reading.

## Recognizing Words in Context

Always check to see whether the words around an unfamiliar word—its context—can give you a clue to the word's meaning.

Suppose, for example, that you are unsure of the meaning of the word *expired* in the following passage:

> Vera wanted to check out a book, but her library card had expired. She had to borrow my card because she didn't have time to renew hers.

You could begin to figure out the meaning of *expired* by asking yourself a question such as, What could have happened to Vera's library card that would make her need to borrow someone else's card? You might realize that if Vera had to renew her card, its usefulness must have come to an end or run out. This would lead you to conclude that the word *expired* must mean "to come to an end" or "to run out." You would be right. The context suggested the meaning.

Context can also affect the meaning of a word you already know. The word *key*, for instance, has many meanings. There are musical keys, door keys, and keys to solving a mystery. The context in which the word *key* occurs will tell you which meaning is correct.

Sometimes a word is explained by the words that immediately follow it. The subject of a sentence and your knowledge about that subject might also help you determine the meaning of an unknown word. Try to decide the meaning of the word *revive* in the following sentence:

> Sunshine and water will revive those drooping plants.

The compound subject is *sunshine and water*. You know that plants need light and water to survive and that drooping plants are not healthy. You can figure out that *revive* means "to bring back to health."

## Keeping Events in Order

Sequence, or chronological order, is the order of events in a story or the order of steps in a process. Paying attention to the sequence of events or steps will help you follow what is happening, predict what might happen next, and make sense of a passage.

To make the sequence as clear as possible, writers often use signal words to help the reader get a more exact idea of when things happen. Following is a list of frequently used signal words and phrases:

| | |
|---|---|
| until | first |
| next | then |
| before | after |
| finally | later |
| when | while |
| during | now |
| at the end | by the time |
| as soon as | in the beginning |

Signal words and phrases are also useful when a writer chooses to relate details or events out of sequence. You need to pay careful attention to determine the correct chronological order.

## Making Evaluations

Evaluating is making judgments or forming opinions about what you are reading and how it is presented. When you evaluate, you are using your personal understanding and ideas to help you understand the story.

To make an evaluation, think about your reaction to what happens in a passage. Consider the way the author presents the characters and information. Ask yourself, What do I think about what I just read? To answer this question, you will need to draw on your prior knowledge and experiences as well as on your personal beliefs and ideas.

Look at the following passage:

Isabel frowned and moaned when the nanny turned away. The six-year-old kicked her shoe, then the sock, off her foot. The nanny sighed and collected the scattered pieces. She was growing more and more weary of Isabel's stubborn behavior.

After reading the passage, you might make the evaluation *Isabel is a spoiled child*. But someone else might make a different evaluation, such as *The nanny does not give Isabel enough attention*. Both evaluations are judgments that are supported by the information in the passage.

It is important to know the difference between an evaluation and a statement that comes directly from the text. A person who reads the passage and says, "The nanny is getting tired," is not making an evaluation. The person is simply restating the information that is already provided in the text without making a judgment or forming an opinion about characters, places, or events that goes beyond the text.

As you read, be aware of the evaluations that you make about characters, places, and events that the author describes.

## Making Correct Inferences

Much of what you read *suggests* more than it *says*. Writers often do not state ideas directly in a text. They can't. Think of the time and space it would take to state every idea. And think of how boring that would be! Instead, writers leave it to you, the reader, to fill in the information they leave out—to make inferences. You do this by combining clues in the text with knowledge from your own experience.

You make many inferences every day. Suppose, for example, that you are visiting a friend's house. You see several suitcases near the door. You infer (make an inference) that your neighbor is about to go on a trip. Another day you overhear a conversation. You catch the names of two actors and the words *scene, dialogue,* and *directing.* You infer that the people are discussing a movie or a play.

In these situations and others like them, you infer unstated information from what you observe or read. Readers must make inferences in order to understand text.

Be careful about the inferences you make. One set of facts may suggest several inferences. Some of these inferences could be faulty. A good inference is always supported by sound evidence, or facts and clues that show something to be true.

Remember the suitcases that caused you to infer that your neighbor had plans to travel? That could be a faulty inference. Perhaps your neighbor isn't planning to travel at all. Perhaps the suitcases are there because he or she is going to lend them to a friend. To make a more accurate inference, you would need to look for more evidence.

## Summarizing

A summary is a shortened version of a text that includes only the most important ideas in the text. A summary should provide the overall idea of what happens in the passage. A summary does not include any details unnecessary to the overall understanding of the passage. While details are necessary in the story for the reader to enjoy and connect to the story in depth, details are not necessary in a summary.

Look at the following passage and its summary:

Henry and Jordan ran faster and faster. The sound of the train whistle grew sharp in their ears as they approached the station. As the conductor called "All aboard!" in his deep, confident voice, they slipped through the crowd and across the platform and leapt through the closest open door. They had made it! At last they were on their way to Spain.

Summary: *Henry and Jordan run to catch a train to Spain right before it leaves the station.*

This passage describes an event that two characters experience. The summary shown above includes the names of the two characters, what they do, and why they do it. The details about the conductor's voice and the train whistle, for example, are not included in the summary.

As you read the following passage, try to find the most important ideas. Then review the summary.

> The sun shone brightly over the meadow and soon burned off the morning haze. I watched anxiously as Latricia rode faster and faster over the ground, her horse's hooves throwing up clumps of loose sod into the damp air. Latricia's hair flew behind her in a constant wave, as if to bid me good day. They approached the first jump, and I held my breath.

Summary: *The narrator watches anxiously as Latricia rides her horse across the meadow toward the first jump.*

Notice how the summary includes the characters, what they do, and how the narrator feels. It does not include details about how the horse runs or the way Latricia's hair moves. These details are not necessary for understanding the most important ideas in the passage.

Knowing how to summarize is an important skill. It can help you check your understanding as you read and remember the most important parts of the story.

# Working Through a Lesson

## Part A

1. **Preview the passage.** Locate the timed selection in Part A of the lesson that you are going to read. Wait for your teacher's signal to preview. You will have 20 seconds for previewing. Follow the previewing steps described on pages 2 and 3.

2. **Read the passage.** When your teacher gives you the signal, begin reading. Read carefully so that you will be able to answer questions about what you have read. Your teacher will be writing times on the chalkboard. When you finish reading, look at the chalkboard and note your reading time. Write this time at the bottom of the page on the line labeled Reading Time.

3. **Complete the exercises.** Answer the 10 questions that follow the passage. There are five fact questions and five idea questions. Put an X in the box next to the best answer for each question.

4. **Correct your work.** Use the Answer Key at the back of the book to check your answers. Circle any wrong answer and put an X in the box you should have marked. Record the number of your correct answers for Part A in the space provided on the last page of the lesson.

## Part B

1. **Preview and read the passage.** Use the same techniques you use to read Part A. Think carefully about the meaning of the passage.

2. **Complete the exercises.** There are five activities that help you practice five different skills. Instructions are given for completing each activity. Each activity has three responses, so there are 15 total responses for you to record in Part B.

3. **Correct your work.** Use the Answer Key at the back of the book. Circle any wrong answer and write the correct letter or number next to it. Record the number of your correct answers for Part B in the space provided on the last page of the lesson.

## Plotting Your Progress

1. **Find your reading rate.** Turn to the Reading Rate graph on page 116. Put an *X* at the point where the vertical line that represents the lesson intersects your reading time, shown along the left-hand side. The right-hand side of the graph will reveal your words-per-minute reading speed.

2. **Find your comprehension score.** Add your scores for Part A and Part B to determine the total number of your correct answers. Turn to the Comprehension Score Graph on page 117. Put an *X* at the point where the vertical line that represents your lesson intersects your total correct answers, shown along the left-hand side. The right-hand side of the graph will show the percentage of questions you answered correctly.

3. **Complete the Comprehension Skills Profile.** Turn to page 118. Record your incorrect answers for the Part B exercises. The five Part B skills are listed along the bottom. There are five columns of boxes—one column for each question. For every incorrect answer, put an *X* in a box for that skill.

To get the most benefit from these lessons, you need to take charge of your own progress in improving your reading speed and comprehension. Studying these graphs will help you to see whether your reading rate is increasing and to determine what skills you need to work on. Your teacher will also review the graphs to check your progress.

# To the Teacher

## About the Series

*Timed Readings Plus in Literature* includes 10 books at reading levels 4–13, with one book at each level. Book One contains material at a fourth-grade reading level, Book Two at a fifth-grade level, and so on. The readability level is determined by the Fry Readability Scale and is not to be confused with grade level or age. The books are designed for use with students at middle school level and above.

The purposes of the series are

- to provide systematic, structured reading practice that helps students improve their reading rate and comprehension skills;

- to give students experience in reading literature;

- to prepare students for taking standardized tests that include timed reading passages;

- to provide materials with a wide range of reading levels so that students can continue to practice and improve their reading rate and comprehension skills.

Each book in the series contains 25 two-part lessons. Part A focuses on improving reading rate. This section of the lesson consists of a 400-word timed literature passage followed by two multiple-choice exercises. Recalling Facts includes five fact questions; Understanding Ideas includes five critical thinking questions.

Part B concentrates on building mastery in critical areas of comprehension. This section consists of a non-timed passage—the "plus" passage—followed by five exercises that address five major comprehension skills. The passage varies in length but is generally about 200 words long.

## Timed Reading and Comprehension

Timed reading is the best-known method of improving reading speed. However, there is no point in having a student read at an accelerated speed if the student does not understand what she or he is reading. Nothing is more important than comprehension in reading.

Few students will be able to read a passage once and answer all of the questions correctly. A score of 70 or 80 percent correct is standard. If a student gets 90 or 100 percent correct, either he or she is reading too slowly or the material is at too low a reading level. A comprehension or critical thinking score of less than 70 percent indicates a need for improvement.

One method of improving comprehension and critical thinking skills is for the student to go back and study each incorrect answer. First the student should reread the question carefully. Many students choose the wrong answer simply because they have not read the question carefully. Then the student should look back in the passage to find the place where the question is answered, reread that part of the passage, and think about how to arrive at the correct answer. It is important to be able to recognize the correct answer when it is embedded in the text. Teacher guidance or class discussion will help the student find the answer.

## Speed Versus Comprehension

It is not unusual for comprehension scores to decline as reading rate increases during the early weeks of timed readings. If this happens, students should attempt to level off their speed—but not lower it—and concentrate more on comprehension. Usually, if students maintain the higher speed and concentrate on comprehension, scores will gradually improve and within a week or two be back up to levels of 70 to 80 percent.

It is important to achieve a proper balance between speed and comprehension. An inefficient reader typically reads everything at one speed, usually slowly. Some poor readers, however, read rapidly but without satisfactory comprehension. It is important to achieve a balance between speed and comprehension. The practice that this series provides enables students to increase their reading speed while maintaining standard levels of comprehension.

## Getting Started

Begin by assigning students to a level. A student should start with a book that is one level below his or her current reading level. If a student's reading level is not known, a suitable starting point would be one or two levels below the student's present grade in school.

Introduce students to the contents and format of the book they are using. Examine the book to see how it is organized. Talk about the parts of each lesson. Discuss the purpose of timed reading and the use of the progress graphs at the back of the book.

## Timing the Reading

One suggestion for timing the reading is to have all students begin reading the selection at the same time. After one minute, write on the board the time that has elapsed and begin updating it at 10-second intervals (1:00, 1:10, 1:20, etc.). Another option is to have individual students time themselves with a stopwatch.

## Teaching a Lesson

### Part A

1. Give students the signal to begin previewing the lesson. Allow 20 seconds.

2. Use one of the methods described above to time students as they read the passage. (Include the 20-second preview time as part of the first minute.) Tell students to write down the last time shown on the board or the stopwatch when they finish reading. Have them record the time in the designated space after the passage.

3. Have students complete the exercises in Part A. Work with them to check their answers, using the Answer Key, which begins on page 114. Have them circle incorrect answers, mark the correct answers, and then record the number of correct answers for Part A on the appropriate line at the end of the lesson. Correct responses to eight or more questions indicate satisfactory comprehension and recall.

### Part B

1. Have students read the Part B passage and complete the exercises that follow it. Directions are provided with each exercise. Correct responses require deliberation and discrimination.

2. Work with students to check their answers. Then discuss the answers with them and have them record the number of correct answers for Part B at the end of the lesson.

3. Have students study the correct answers to the questions they answered incorrectly. It is important that they understand why a particular answer is correct or incorrect. Have them reread relevant parts of a passage to clarify an answer. An effective cooperative activity is to have students work in pairs to discuss their answers, explain why they chose the answers they did, and try to resolve differences.

## Monitoring Progress

Have students find their total correct answers for the lesson and record their reading time and scores on the graphs on pages 116 and 117. Then have them complete the Comprehension Skills Profile on page 118. For each incorrect response to a question in Part B, students should mark an X in the box above each question type.

The legend on the Reading Rate graph automatically converts reading times to words-per-minute rates. The Comprehension Score graph automatically converts the raw scores to percentages.

These graphs provide a visual record of a student's progress. This record gives the student and you an opportunity to evaluate the student's progress and to determine the types of exercises and skills he or she needs to concentrate on.

## Diagnosis and Evaluation

The following are typical reading rates:

Slow Reader—150 Words Per Minute

Average Reader—250 Words Per Minute

Fast Reader—350 Words Per Minute

A student who consistently reads at an average or above-average rate (with satisfactory comprehension) is ready to advance to the next book in the series.

A column of $X$'s in the Comprehension Skills Profile indicates a specific comprehension weakness. Using the profile, you can assess trends in student performance and suggest remedial work if necessary.

# 1   A   *from* **The Wind in the Willows**
## *by Kenneth Grahame*

After they had chatted for a time about things in general, the Badger said, "Now, then! Tell us the news from your part of the world. How's old Toad going on?"

"O, from bad to worse," said the Rat gravely, while the Mole, basking in the firelight, his heels higher than his head, tried to look properly mournful. "Another smashup only last week, and a bad one. You see, he will insist on driving himself, and he's hopelessly incapable. If he'd only employ a steady, well-trained animal, pay him good wages, and leave things to him, he'd get on all right. But no, he's convinced he's a heaven-born driver, and nobody can teach him anything. All the rest follows."

"How many has he had?" asked the Badger.

"Smashes, or machines?" asked the Rat. "O, well, after all, it's the same thing—with Toad. This is the seventh. As for the others—you know that coach house of his? Well, it's piled up—piled up to the roof—with fragments of cars none of them bigger than your hat! That accounts for the other six—as far as they can be accounted for."

"He's been in the hospital three times," put in the Mole. "And as for the fines he's had to pay, it's simply awful to think of."

"Yes, and that's part of the trouble," said the Rat. "Toad's rich, we all know; but he's not a millionaire. And he's such a bad driver, and quite regardless of law and order. Killed or ruined—it's got to be one of the two things, sooner or later. Badger! We're his friends—oughtn't we do something?"

The Badger went through a bit of hard thinking. "Now look here!" he said at last. "Of course you know I can't do anything now?"

His two friends assented, quite understanding his point. No animal is ever expected to do anything heroic, or even moderately active during the off-season of winter. All are sleepy—some actually sleep. All are weather-bound, more or less; and all are resting from arduous days and nights, during which every muscle in them had been sorely tested.

"Very well then!" said the Badger. "But, once the year has really turned, and the nights are shorter—you know!"

Both animals nodded gravely. They knew!

"Well, then," went on the Badger, "we'll take Toad in hand. We'll stand no nonsense at all."

**Reading Time** _____

## Recalling Facts

1. The Toad is a very bad
   - ❏ a. actor.
   - ❏ b. driver.
   - ❏ c. collector.

2. Toad keeps fragments of his old cars in his
   - ❏ a. front yard.
   - ❏ b. coach house.
   - ❏ c. living room.

3. Toad has been in the hospital
   - ❏ a. once.
   - ❏ b. three times.
   - ❏ c. seven times.

4. Toad is
   - ❏ a. poor.
   - ❏ b. stingy.
   - ❏ c. rich.

5. The Badger cannot help Toad during the
   - ❏ a. summer.
   - ❏ b. spring.
   - ❏ c. winter.

## Understanding the Passage

6. The Badger, Mole, and Rat all want to
   - ❏ a. meet Toad.
   - ❏ b. avoid Toad.
   - ❏ c. help Toad.

7. Toad's friends fear for his
   - ❏ a. safety.
   - ❏ b. machines.
   - ❏ c. manners.

8. Toad apparently does not
   - ❏ a. learn from his mistakes.
   - ❏ b. have a driver's license.
   - ❏ c. care how his friends feel.

9. The season this scene takes place in is
   - ❏ a. summer.
   - ❏ b. winter.
   - ❏ c. spring.

10. Toad can best be described as
    - ❏ a. shy.
    - ❏ b. stubborn.
    - ❏ c. lonely.

# 1 B   *from* **Jane Eyre**
### *by Charlotte Brontë*

I heard the front door open; Mr. Bates came out, and with him was a nurse. After she had seen him mount his horse and depart, she was about to close the door, but I ran up to her.

"How is Helen Burns?"

"Very poorly," was the answer.

"Is it her Mr. Bates has been to see?"

"Yes."

"And what does he say about her?"

"He says she'll not be here long."

This phrase, uttered in my hearing yesterday, would have only conveyed the notion that she was about to be removed to Northumberland, to her own home. I should not have suspected that it meant she was dying. But I knew instantly now: it was clear that Helen Burns was numbering her last days in this world, and that she was going to be taken to the region of spirits, if such region there were. I experienced a shock of horror, then a strong thrill of grief, then a desire—a necessity to see her. I asked in what room she lay.

"She is in Miss Temple's room," said the nurse.

1. **Recognizing Words in Context**

   Find the word *uttered* in the passage. One definition below is closest to the meaning of that word. One definition has the opposite or nearly the opposite meaning. The remaining definition has a completely different meaning. Label each definition C for *closest*, O for *opposite or nearly opposite*, or D for *different*.

   _____ a. thought

   _____ b. spoken

   _____ c. decided

2. **Keeping Events in Order**

   Number each statement below 1, 2, or 3 to show the order in which the events took place.

   _____ a. The narrator sees Mr. Bates leave on his horse.

   _____ b. The narrator feels a desire to see Helen Burns.

   _____ c. The narrator runs up to the nurse.

## 3. Making Evaluations

Two of the statements below describe things that actually happen or are stated in the passage. The other statement is an evaluation, or a judgment or opinion, about a character, setting, or event in the passage. Label each statement E for *evaluation* or H for *happens or is stated in the passage.*

_____ a. The narrator knows Helen Burns is dying.

_____ b. Mr. Bates visits Helen Burns.

_____ c. The narrator is a caring person.

## 4. Making Correct Inferences

Two of the statements below are correct inferences, or reasonable guesses. They are based on information in the passage. The other statement is an incorrect, or faulty, inference. Label each statement C for *correct* inference or F for *faulty* inference.

_____ a. The narrator has a close relationship with Helen Burns.

_____ b. The narrator is afraid of Mr. Bates.

_____ c. Mr. Bates has some medical knowledge.

## 5. Summarizing

One of the statements below is a summary that tells the most important ideas in the passage. The other two statements contain details from the passage. They do not tell the most important ideas in the passage. Label each statement S for *summary* or D for *details.*

_____ a. Mr. Bates leaves the building along with a nurse.

_____ b. The narrator experiences a shock of horror and then a desire to see Helen Burns.

_____ c. The narrator speaks with a nurse and realizes that Helen Burns is dying.

Correct Answers, Part A _____

Correct Answers, Part B _____

Total Correct Answers _____

*from* **Heidi**

*by Johanna Spyri*

Dete stood still. A stout, kind-looking woman came out of the house and joined them. "Where are you taking the child, Dete?" she asked. "I suppose your sister's child—the orphan?"

"Yes," answered Dete. "I am taking her to stay with Alm-Uncle."

"Surely you aren't going to leave the child with *him*. You must be out of your mind, Dete! But the old man is sure to turn you away, in any case!"

"He can't do that! After all, he is her grandfather. I have looked after the child up till now, and I can tell you, Barbel, I am not going to turn down the offer of a good job on her account. From now on the grandfather will have to do his bit as well."

"Oh, well, if he were like other people—" replied Barbel, "but you know him as well as I do. How can he look after a child, and especially such a little one? Oh, she will never stay with him! But where are *you* going, Dete?"

"To a very good job in Frankfurt," explained Dete.

"Well, I certainly wouldn't like to be the child," said Barbel disapprovingly. "Nobody knows anything about the old man up there. He never speaks to anybody. With his bushy eyebrows and terrible beard he looks a positive savage. The whole village is afraid of him."

"Still," Dete persisted, "he is the grandfather and it's up to him to look after the child."

"They say all sorts of terrible things about the old man," said Barbel, glancing keenly at her companion. "You must surely have heard his history from your sister, eh, Dete?"

"Perhaps I have, but I shan't say. It would be a fine thing for me if he found out I had been talking!"

Barbel had been eager for a long time to learn something about the old man called Alm-Uncle. She wanted to know why he seemed to hate everybody and why he lived all by himself up on the mountain. Confidentially she took Dete's arm. "Do tell me, now! You have nothing to fear," she coaxed.

Dete looked round to see whether the child was nearby and might hear what she had to say, but the little one was not in sight. Frightened, Dete stopped in some consternation, and looked back. There was no sign of the child.

**Reading Time** _____

## Recalling Facts

1. The child is
   - ❏ a. very sickly.
   - ❏ b. an orphan.
   - ❏ c. a stepson.

2. Alm-Uncle is the child's
   - ❏ a. uncle.
   - ❏ b. granduncle.
   - ❏ c. grandfather.

3. Dete has just gotten a
   - ❏ a. good job.
   - ❏ b. new house.
   - ❏ c. new husband.

4. Barbel feels sorry for
   - ❏ a. Alm-Uncle.
   - ❏ b. the child.
   - ❏ c. herself.

5. Alm-Uncle
   - ❏ a. is wealthy.
   - ❏ b. is the mayor of the town.
   - ❏ c. lives by himself.

## Understanding the Passage

6. Barbel thinks that Alm-Uncle will
   - ❏ a. refuse to take the child.
   - ❏ b. welcome the child with open arms.
   - ❏ c. take a job in another town.

7. Dete took care of the orphan
   - ❏ a. out of a sense of duty.
   - ❏ b. because she loved her so much.
   - ❏ c. because her sister paid her.

8. Alm-Uncle frightens people because of the way he
   - ❏ a. talks.
   - ❏ b. works.
   - ❏ c. looks.

9. Dete feels sure that
   - ❏ a. Alm-Uncle will make a good parent.
   - ❏ b. the child will love Alm-Uncle.
   - ❏ c. Alm-Uncle will take in the child.

10. Barbel wants to
    - ❏ a. take the child herself.
    - ❏ b. hear more gossip.
    - ❏ c. take a job in Frankfurt.

## 2 B  *from* The Adventures of Huckleberry Finn

### *by Mark Twain*

I set the candle down. I noticed the window was up; so he had clumb in by the shed. He kept a-looking me all over. By and by he says:

"Starchy clothes—very. You think you're a good deal of a big-bug, *don't* you?"

"Maybe I am, maybe I ain't," I says.

"Don't you give me none o' your lip," says he. "You've put on considerable many frills since I been away. I'll take you down a peg before I get done with you. You're educated, too, they say—can read and write. You think you're better'n your father, now, don't you, because he can't? *I'll* take it out of you. Who told you you might meddle with such highfalutin foolishness, hey? Who told you you could?"

"The widow. She told me."

"The widow, hey? And who told the widow she could put in her shovel about a thing that ain't none of her business?"

"Nobody never told her."

"Well, I'll learn her how to meddle. And looky here—you drop that school, you hear? I'll learn people to bring up a boy to put on airs over his own father and let on to be better'n what *he* is."

1. **Recognizing Words in Context**

   Find the word *meddle* in the passage. One definition below is closest to the meaning of that word. One definition has the opposite or nearly the opposite meaning. The remaining definition has a completely different meaning. Label each definition C for *closest*, O for *opposite or nearly opposite*, or D for *different*.

   _____ a. leave something alone

   _____ b. create

   _____ c. interfere

2. **Keeping Events in Order**

   Number each statement below 1, 2, or 3 to show the order in which the events took place.

   _____ a. Huck's father climbs in through the window.

   _____ b. The widow tells Huck that he could learn to read and write.

   _____ c. Huck's father tells Huck to stop going to school.

3. **Making Evaluations**

   Two of the statements below describe things that actually happen or are stated in the passage. The other statement is an evaluation, or a judgment or opinion, about a character, setting, or event in the passage. Label each statement E for *evaluation* or H for *happens or is stated in the passage.*

   _____ a. Huck's father looks him over.

   _____ b. Huck's father is not a good father.

   _____ c. Huck's father cannot read or write.

4. **Making Correct Inferences**

   Two of the statements below are correct inferences, or reasonable guesses. They are based on information in the passage. The other statement is an incorrect, or faulty, inference. Label each statement C for *correct* inference or F for *faulty* inference.

   _____ a. The widow thinks that a good education is important.

   _____ b. Huck's father has been away for a while.

   _____ c. Huck wishes that he had not learned to read and write.

5. **Summarizing**

   One of the statements below is a summary that tells the most important ideas in the passage. The other two statements contain details from the passage. They do not tell the most important ideas in the passage. Label each statement S for *summary* or D for *details.*

   _____ a. Huck's father notices that Huck's clothes are starchy.

   _____ b. Huck's father is upset that Huck has learned to read and write.

   _____ c. Huck's father asks Huck who told him that he could learn.

Correct Answers, Part A _____

Correct Answers, Part B _____

Total Correct Answers _____

## 3 | A | *from* **Rebecca**
### *by Daphne du Maurier*

Maxim had to go up to London at the end of June to some public dinner. A man's dinner. Something to do with the county. He was away for two days and I was left alone. I dreaded his going. When I saw the car disappear round the sweep in the drive I felt exactly as though it were to be a final parting and I should never see him again. There would be an accident of course and later on in the afternoon, when I came back from my walk, I should find Frith, white and frightened, waiting for me with a message. The doctor would have rung up from some cottage hospital. "You must be very brave," he would say, "I am afraid you must be prepared for a great shock."

And Frank would come, and we would go to the hospital together. Maxim would not recognize me. I went through the whole thing as I was sitting at lunch, I could see the crowd of local people clustering round the churchyard at the funeral, and myself leaning on Frank's arm. It was so real to me that I could scarcely eat any lunch, and I kept straining my ears to hear the telephone should it ring.

I sat out in the garden under the chestnut tree in the afternoon, with a book on my lap, but I scarcely read at all. When I saw Robert come across the lawn I knew it was the telephone and I felt physically sick. "A message from the club, Madam, to say Mr. de Winter arrived ten minutes ago."

I shut up my book. "Thank you, Robert. How quickly he got up."

"Yes, Madam. A very good run."

"Did he ask to speak to me, or leave any special message?"

"No, Madam. Just that he had arrived safely. It was the porter speaking."

"All right, Robert. Thanks very much."

The relief was tremendous. I did not feel sick anymore. The pain had gone. It was like coming ashore after a channel crossing. I began to feel rather hungry, and when Robert had gone back into the house I crept into the dining room through the long window and stole some biscuits from the sideboard. I took six of them. And then an apple as well. I had no idea I was so empty. I went and ate them in the woods.

**Reading Time** _____

## Recalling Facts

1. Maxim is going to be away for
   - ❑ a. two hours.
   - ❑ b. two days.
   - ❑ c. three weeks.

2. Maxim's trip makes the narrator
   - ❑ a. happy.
   - ❑ b. relieved.
   - ❑ c. miserable.

3. The narrator imagines that Maxim will
   - ❑ a. run away for good.
   - ❑ b. have an accident and die.
   - ❑ c. return before the dinner.

4. The narrator gets a message stating that
   - ❑ a. Robert has arrived.
   - ❑ b. Mr. de Winter has made it to the club.
   - ❑ c. Maxim will be late.

5. After receiving the message, the narrator eats
   - ❑ a. some biscuits and an apple.
   - ❑ b. six small apples.
   - ❑ c. two biscuits with jam.

## Understanding the Passage

6. The narrator has a
   - ❑ a. desire to travel.
   - ❑ b. constant stomachache.
   - ❑ c. lively imagination.

7. Frith and Robert appear to be
   - ❑ a. family servants.
   - ❑ b. close family friends.
   - ❑ c. local doctors.

8. The narrator is apparently
   - ❑ a. poor.
   - ❑ b. just a young child.
   - ❑ c. fairly rich.

9. Mr. de Winter's first name must be
   - ❑ a. Robert
   - ❑ b. Maxim.
   - ❑ c. Frank.

10. The message from the porter makes the narrator
    - ❑ a. relax.
    - ❑ b. nervous.
    - ❑ c. upset.

## 3 B from **Black Beauty**

*by Anna Sewell*

The doctor came out with his riding-whip.

"You need not take that, sir," said John; "Black Beauty will go till he drops. Take care of him, sir, if you can; I should not like any harm to come to him."

"No, no, John," said the doctor, "I hope not," and in a minute we had left John far behind.

I will not tell you about our way back. The doctor was a heavier man than John, and not so good a rider; however, I did my very best. The man at the tollgate had it open. When we came to the hill the doctor drew me up. "Now, my good fellow," he said, "take some breath." I was glad he did, for I was nearly spent, but that breathing helped me on, and soon we were in the park. Joe was at the lodge gate; my master was at the hall door, for he had heard us coming. He spoke not a word; the doctor went into the house with him, and Joe led me to the stable. I was glad to get home; my legs shook under me, and I could only stand and pant. I had not a dry hair on my body, and water ran down my legs.

1. **Recognizing Words in Context**

   Find the word *spent* in the passage. One definition below is closest to the meaning of that word. One definition has the opposite or nearly the opposite meaning. The remaining definition has a completely different meaning. Label each definition C for *closest,* O for *opposite or nearly opposite,* or D for *different.*

   _____ a. exhausted

   _____ b. full of energy

   _____ c. angry

2. **Keeping Events in Order**

   Number each statement below 1, 2, or 3 to show the order in which the events took place.

   _____ a. John tells the doctor to take good care of Black Beauty.

   _____ b. Joe leads Black Beauty to the stable.

   _____ c. Black Beauty and the doctor pass through the tollgate.

## 3. Making Evaluations

Two of the statements below describe things that actually happen or are stated in the passage. The other statement is an evaluation, or a judgment or opinion, about a character, setting, or event in the passage. Label each statement E for *evaluation* or H for *happens or is stated in the passage*.

_____ a. Black Beauty is a hard-working horse.

_____ b. The doctor is heavier than John.

_____ c. The doctor gives Black Beauty a chance to stop and breathe.

## 4. Making Correct Inferences

Two of the statements below are correct inferences, or reasonable guesses. They are based on information in the passage. The other statement is an incorrect, or faulty, inference. Label each statement C for *correct* inference or F for *faulty* inference.

_____ a. John has ridden Black Beauty before.

_____ b. The doctor has never ridden a horse before.

_____ c. Someone at the master's house needs a doctor.

## 5. Summarizing

One of the statements below is a summary that tells the most important ideas in the passage. The other two statements contain details from the passage. They do not tell the most important ideas in the passage. Label each statement S for *summary* or D for *details*.

_____ a. Black Beauty works hard to get the doctor to his master's house.

_____ b. John believes that Black Beauty will keep going until he drops.

_____ c. Black Beauty is tired, shaky, and sweaty after a long, difficult ride.

Correct Answers, Part A _____

Correct Answers, Part B _____

Total Correct Answers _____

## *from* **The Trimmed Lamp**
### *by O. Henry*

Lou and Nancy waited on the corner for Dan. Dan was Lou's steady company.

"Ain't you cold Nance?" said Lou. "Say, what a chump you are for working in that old store for $8 a week! I made $18.50 last week. Of course ironing ain't as swell work as selling lace behind a counter, but it pays. None of us ironers make less than $10. And I don't know that it's any less respectful work, either."

"You can have it," said Nancy. "I'll take my eight a week and hall bedroom. I like to be among nice things and swell people. And look what a chance I've got! Why, one of our glove girls married a Pittsburg—steel maker, or blacksmith or something—the other day worth a million dollars. I'll catch a swell myself some time. I ain't bragging on my looks or anything but I'll take my chances where there's big prizes offered. What show would a girl have in a laundry?"

"Why, that's where I met Dan," said Lou. "He came in for his Sunday shirt and collars and saw me at the first board, ironing. We all try to get to work at the first board. Ella Maginnis was sick that day, and I had her place. He said he noticed my arms first, how round and white they was. I had my sleeves rolled up. Some nice fellows come into laundries. You can tell 'em by their bringing their clothes in suitcases and turning in the door sharp and sudden."

"How can you wear a waist like that, Lou?" said Nancy, gazing down at the offending article with sweet scorn. "It shows fierce taste."

"This waist?" cried Lou, with wide-eyed indignation. "Why, I paid $16 for this waist. It's worth twenty-five. A woman left it to be laundered, and never called for it. The boss sold it to me. It's got yards and yards of hand embroidery on it. Better talk about that ugly, plain thing you've got on."

"This ugly, plain thing," said Nancy, calmly, "was copied from one that Mrs. Van Alstyne Fisher was wearing. The girls say her bill in the store last year was $12,000. I made mine, myself. It cost me $1.50. Ten feet away you couldn't tell it from hers."

"Oh, well," said Lou, good-naturedly, "if you want to starve and put on airs, go ahead."

**Reading Time** _____

## Recalling Facts

1. Dan is
   - ❏ a. Lou's boyfriend.
   - ❏ b. Nancy's boyfriend.
   - ❏ c. Lou's boss.

2. Nancy works
   - ❏ a. in a laundry room.
   - ❏ b. selling lace.
   - ❏ c. as a blacksmith.

3. Last week Lou earned
   - ❏ a. $10.
   - ❏ b. $8.
   - ❏ c. $18.50.

4. Ella Maginnis was
   - ❏ a. absent from work one day.
   - ❏ b. an outstanding salesperson.
   - ❏ c. a rich lady.

5. Lou said her waist is worth
   - ❏ a. $25.
   - ❏ b. $16.
   - ❏ c. $1.50.

## Understanding the Passage

6. Lou thinks Nancy should
   - ❏ a. break up with her boyfriend.
   - ❏ b. get a job in the laundry.
   - ❏ c. find more respectful work.

7. The term "catch a swell" refers to
   - ❏ a. becoming an ironer.
   - ❏ b. talking to a rich lady.
   - ❏ c. finding a rich boyfriend.

8. Nancy and Lou expect to meet the men in their lives
   - ❏ a. at home.
   - ❏ b. at work.
   - ❏ c. while on vacation.

9. Nancy and Lou pay great attention to their
   - ❏ a. weight.
   - ❏ b. age.
   - ❏ c. clothes.

10. Apparently, Nancy and Lou come from
    - ❏ a. rich families.
    - ❏ b. poor families.
    - ❏ c. broken families.

## 4 · B — *from* **The Rocking-Horse Winner**
### *by D. H. Lawrence*

It was about one o'clock when Paul's mother and father drove up to their house. All was still. Paul's mother went to her room and slipped off her white fur cloak. She heard her husband downstairs, mixing a whiskey and soda.

And then, because of the strange anxiety at her heart, she stole upstairs to her son's room. Noiselessly she went along the upper corridor. Was there a faint noise? What was it? She stood, with arrested muscles, outside his door, listening. There was a strange, heavy, and yet not loud noise. Her heart stood still. It was a soundless noise, yet rushing and powerful. Something huge, in angry, hushed motion. What was it? What in God's name was it? She ought to know. She felt that she knew the noise; she knew what it was.

Yet she could not place it; she couldn't say what it was. And on and on it went, like a madness.

Softly, frozen with anxiety and fear, she turned the door handle.

The room was dark. Yet in the space near the window, she heard and saw something plunging to and fro. She gazed in fear and amazement.

---

1. **Recognizing Words in Context**

   Find the word *arrested* in the passage. One definition below is closest to the meaning of that word. One definition has the opposite or nearly the opposite meaning. The remaining definition has a completely different meaning. Label each definition C for *closest*, O for *opposite or nearly opposite*, or D for *different*.

   _____ a. feeling worried

   _____ b. moving quickly

   _____ c. holding still

2. **Keeping Events in Order**

   Number each statement below 1, 2, or 3 to show the order in which the events took place.

   _____ a. Paul's mother sees something plunging to and fro.

   _____ b. Paul's mother takes off her white fur cloak.

   _____ c. Paul's mother hears a strange noise.

3. **Making Evaluations**

Two of the statements below describe things that actually happen or are stated in the passage. The other statement is an evaluation, or a judgment or opinion, about a character, setting, or event in the passage. Label each statement E for *evaluation* or H for *happens or is stated in the passage*.

_____ a. Paul's mother listens outside his room.

_____ b. Paul's mother feels a strange anxiety.

_____ c. Paul's mother gets worried too easily.

4. **Making Correct Inferences**

Two of the statements below are correct inferences, or reasonable guesses. They are based on information in the passage. The other statement is an incorrect, or faulty, inference. Label each statement C for *correct* inference or F for *faulty* inference.

_____ a. Paul's parents do not get along very well.

_____ b. Paul's family is somewhat wealthy.

_____ c. Paul's mother feels deep concern for her son.

5. **Summarizing**

One of the statements below is a summary that tells the most important ideas in the passage. The other two statements contain details from the passage. They do not tell the most important ideas in the passage. Label each statement S for *summary* or D for *details*.

_____ a. Paul's mother hears her husband mixing a drink downstairs.

_____ b. Paul's mother slowly opens the door to Paul's room when she hears noise.

_____ c. Paul's mother feels anxious, so she checks her son's room.

Correct Answers, Part A _____

Correct Answers, Part B _____

Total Correct Answers _____

# *from* **Five Out of One Shell**
## *by Hans Christian Andersen*

There were five peas in one shell: they were green, and the pod was green. So they thought all the world was green, and that was just as it should be! The shell grew, and the peas grew; they accommodated themselves to circumstances, sitting all in a row. The sun shone without, and warmed the husk, and the rain made it clear and transparent; it was mild and agreeable in the bright day and in the dark night, just as it should be, and the peas as they sat there became bigger and bigger, and more and more thoughtful, for something they must do.

"Are we to sit here everlastingly?" asked one. "I'm afraid we shall become hard by long sitting. It seems to me there must be something outside. I have a kind of inkling of it."

And weeks went by. The peas became yellow, and the pod also.

"All the world's turning yellow," said they. And they had a right to say it.

Suddenly they felt a tug at the shell. The shell was torn off, passed through human hands, and glided down into the pocket of a jacket, in company with other full pods.

"Now we shall soon be opened!" they said; and that is just what they were waiting for.

"I should like to know who of us will get farthest!" said the smallest of the five. "Yes, now it will soon show itself."

"What is to be will be," said the biggest.

"Crack!" the pod burst open, and all the five peas rolled out into the bright sunshine. There they lay in a child's hand. A little boy was clutching them, and said they were fine peas for his peashooter. He put one in directly and shot it out.

"Now I'm flying out into the wide world, catch me if you can!" And he was gone.

"I," said the second. "I shall fly straight into the sun. That's a shell worth looking at, and one that exactly suits me." And away he went.

"We'll go to sleep wherever we arrive," said the next two, "but we shall roll on all the same." And they certainly rolled and tumbled down on the ground before they got into the peashooter; but they were put in for all that. "We shall go farthest," said they.

"What is to happen will happen," said the last, as he was shot forth out of the peashooter.

**Reading Time** _____

## Recalling Facts

1. In all, there are
   - ❏ a. four peas.
   - ❏ b. five peas.
   - ❏ c. six peas.

2. The peas fear that long sitting will make them
   - ❏ a. hard.
   - ❏ b. soft.
   - ❏ c. shrivel.

3. After several weeks, the peas turn
   - ❏ a. brown.
   - ❏ b. white.
   - ❏ c. yellow.

4. After being picked, the peas are
   - ❏ a. used to make soup.
   - ❏ b. cooked and served.
   - ❏ c. shot out of a peashooter.

5. The second pea wants to go to the
   - ❏ a. garden.
   - ❏ b. sun.
   - ❏ c. kitchen.

## Understanding the Passage

6. The peas' view of the world is
   - ❏ a. very limited.
   - ❏ b. like a child's.
   - ❏ c. very broad.

7. As the peas get older, they begin to
   - ❏ a. grow lazy.
   - ❏ b. ask more questions.
   - ❏ c. move inside the pod.

8. When the pod is picked, the peas
   - ❏ a. are bruised.
   - ❏ b. are pleased.
   - ❏ c. cry.

9. The pea most willing to accept things as they are is the
   - ❏ a. biggest pea.
   - ❏ b. middle pea.
   - ❏ c. smallest pea.

10. The peas are curious about the
   - ❏ a. color of flowers.
   - ❏ b. distance they will travel.
   - ❏ c. boy's age.

## 5 B from **Uncle Tom's Cabin**

### *by Harriet Beecher Stowe*

"Is he a slave-trader?" said Mrs. Shelby, noticing a certain embarrassment in her husband's manner.

"Why, my dear, what put that into your head?" said Shelby, looking up.

"Nothing—only Eliza came in here after dinner in a great worry, crying and taking on, and said you were talking with a trader, and that she heard him make an offer for her boy—the ridiculous little goose!"

"She did, eh?" said Mr. Shelby, returning to his paper, which he seemed for a few moments quite intent upon, not perceiving that he was holding it bottom upwards.

"It will have to come out," said he, mentally; "as well now as ever."

"I told Eliza," said Mrs. Shelby, as she continued brushing her hair, "that she was a little fool for her pains, and that you never had anything to do with that sort of person. Of course, I knew you never meant to sell any of our people—least of all, to such a fellow."

"Well, Emily," said her husband, "so I have always felt and said; but the fact is, my business lies so that I cannot get on without. I shall have to sell some of my hands."

1. **Recognizing Words in Context**

   Find the word *perceiving* in the passage. One definition below is closest to the meaning of that word. One definition has the opposite or nearly the opposite meaning. The remaining definition has a completely different meaning. Label each definition C for *closest*, O for *opposite or nearly opposite*, or D for *different*.

   _____ a. ignoring

   _____ b. noticing

   _____ c. caring

2. **Keeping Events in Order**

   Number each statement below 1, 2, or 3 to show the order in which the events took place.

   _____ a. Mr. Shelby tells his wife that he must sell some of his hands.

   _____ b. Mrs. Shelby tells Eliza that she is being foolish.

   _____ c. Eliza cries to Mrs. Shelby about a trader talking to Mr. Shelby.

## 3. Making Evaluations

Two of the statements below describe things that actually happen or are stated in the passage. The other statement is an evaluation, or a judgment or opinion, about a character, setting, or event in the passage. Label each statement E for *evaluation* or H for *happens or is stated in the passage*.

_____ a. Eliza thinks that Mr. Shelby wants to sell her son.

_____ b. Mr. and Mrs. Shelby should not buy and sell people.

_____ c. Mrs. Shelby notices that her husband is embarrassed.

## 4. Making Correct Inferences

Two of the statements below are correct *inferences*, or reasonable guesses. They are based on information in the passage. The other statement is an incorrect, or faulty, inference. Label the statements C for *correct* inference and F for *faulty* inference.

_____ a. Mr. Shelby wishes he did not have to sell any of his hands.

_____ b. Mrs. Shelby does not approve of the trader.

_____ c. Eliza often overhears Mr. Shelby's conversations.

## 5. Summarizing

One of the statements below is a summary that tells the most important ideas in the passage. The other two statements contain details from the passage. They do not tell the most important ideas in the passage. Label each statement S for *summary* or D for *details*.

_____ a. Much to his wife's surprise, Mr. Shelby decides he must sell some of his hands to save his business.

_____ b. Eliza becomes upset when she overhears a trader making an offer for her son to Mr. Shelby.

_____ c. Mrs. Shelby doesn't think that her husband would ever deal with that kind of trader.

Correct Answers, Part A _____

Correct Answers, Part B _____

Total Correct Answers _____

# *from* **The House of Pride**
### *by Jack London*

"Do you wonder that I lost my heart to Kona eighteen years ago?" Cudworth demanded. "I could never leave it now. I think I should die. It would be terrible. There was another man who loved it, even as I. I think he loved it more, for he was born here on the Kona coast. He was a great man, my best friend, my more than brother. But he left it, and he did not die."

"Love?" I queried. "A woman?"

Cudworth shook his head. "Nor will he ever come back, though his heart will be here until he dies."

He paused and gazed down upon the beachlights of Kailua. I smoked silently and waited.

"He was already in love . . . with his wife. Also, he had three children, and he loved them. They are in Honolulu now. The boy is going to college."

"Some rash act?" I questioned, after a time, impatiently.

He shook his head. "Not guilty of anything criminal, nor charged with anything criminal. He was the sheriff of Kona."

"You choose to be paradoxical," I said.

"I suppose it does sound that way," he admitted, "and that is the perfect hell of it."

He looked at me searchingly for a moment, and then abruptly took up the tale.

"He was a leper. No, he was not born with it—no one is born with it; it came upon him. This man—what does it matter? Lyte Gregory was his name. Every person who has lived in Hawaii for a long time knows the story. He was straight American stock, but he was built like the chieftains of old Hawaii. He stood six feet three. His stripped weight was two hundred and twenty pounds, not an ounce of which was not clean muscle or bone. He was the strongest man I have ever seen. He was an athlete and a giant. He was a god. He was my friend. And his heart and his soul were as big and as fine as his body.

"I wonder what you would do if you saw your friend, your brother, on the slippery lip of a precipice, slipping, slipping, and you were able to do nothing. That was just it. I could do nothing. I saw it coming, and I could do nothing. My God, man! What could I do? There it was, malignant and incontestable, the mark of the thing on his brow. No one else saw it."

**Reading Time** _____

## Recalling Facts

1. Cudworth has been in love with Kona for
   - ❏ a. eight years.
   - ❏ b. eighteen years.
   - ❏ c. twenty-eight years.

2. Cudworth's friend
   - ❏ a. died on the Kona coast.
   - ❏ b. left Kona.
   - ❏ c. had no family.

3. Cudworth's friend had been
   - ❏ a. a criminal.
   - ❏ b. the sheriff.
   - ❏ c. a pirate.

4. Cudworth's friend
   - ❏ a. was born a leper.
   - ❏ b. developed leprosy.
   - ❏ c. was a Hawaiian chieftain.

5. Cudworth's friend had been
   - ❏ a. a giant of a man.
   - ❏ b. unmarried.
   - ❏ c. an old and frail man.

## Understanding the Passage

6. Cudworth deeply loves
   - ❏ a. Kona.
   - ❏ b. his leper friend.
   - ❏ c. both a and b.

7. Cudworth's friend
   - ❏ a. loved Kona.
   - ❏ b. didn't know about Kona.
   - ❏ c. hated Kona.

8. Gregory's story
   - ❏ a. has never been told.
   - ❏ b. is well known to the narrator.
   - ❏ c. is well known to many people in Hawaii.

9. Lepers
   - ❏ a. are strong and powerful.
   - ❏ b. have a disease.
   - ❏ c. love nature.

10. Cudworth is about to tell
    - ❏ a. what happened to his friend next.
    - ❏ b. a story about Gregory's children.
    - ❏ c. the narrator to leave Kona as soon as possible.

# 6 B from **Victory**

*by Joseph Conrad*

"Listen—I'm not twenty yet. It's the truth, and I can't be so bad looking, or else—I will tell you straight that I have been worried and pestered by fellows like this before. I don't know what comes to them—"

She was speaking hurriedly. She choked, and then exclaimed, with an accent of despair:

"What is it? What's the matter?"

Heyst had removed his arms from her suddenly, and had recoiled a little. "Is it my fault? I didn't even look at them, I tell you straight. Never! Have I looked at you? Tell me. It was you that began it."

In truth, Heyst had shrunk from the idea of competition with fellows unknown, with Schomberg the hotel keeper. The white figure before him swayed pitifully in the darkness. He felt ashamed of his fastidiousness.

"I am afraid we have been detected," he murmured. "I think I saw somebody on the path between the house and the bushes behind you."

He had seen no one. It was a compassionate lie, if there ever was one. His compassion was as genuine as his shrinking had been, and in his judgment more honorable.

She didn't turn her head. She was obviously relieved.

## 1. Recognizing Words in Context

Find the word *detected* in the passage. One definition below is closest to the meaning of that word. One definition has the opposite or nearly the opposite meaning. The remaining definition has a completely different meaning. Label each definition C for *closest*, O for *opposite or nearly opposite*, or D for *different*.

_____ a. overlooked

_____ b. celebrated

_____ c. seen

## 2. Keeping Events in Order

Number each statement below 1, 2, or 3 to show the order in which the events took place.

_____ a. The girl tells Heyst that she has been pestered by fellows before.

_____ b. Heyst removes his arms from the girl.

_____ c. Heyst says that he saw someone on the path.

## 3. Making Evaluations

Two of the statements below describe things that actually happen or are stated in the passage. The other statement is an evaluation, or a judgment or opinion, about a character, setting, or event in the passage. Label each statement E for *evaluation* or H for *happens or is stated in the passage*.

_____ a. Heyst is not a very brave man.

_____ b. Heyst does not like the idea of competition.

_____ c. Heyst tells a lie to the girl.

## 4. Making Correct Inferences

Two of the statements below are correct inferences, or reasonable guesses. They are based on information in the passage. The other statement is an incorrect, or faulty, inference. Label each statement C for *correct* inference or F for *faulty* inference.

_____ a. Schomberg the hotel keeper is also interested in the girl.

_____ b. Heyst has known the girl for many years.

_____ c. The girl prefers Heyst to the other fellows.

## 5. Summarizing

One of the statements below is a summary that tells the most important ideas in the passage. The other two statements contain details from the passage. They do not tell the most important ideas in the passage. Label each statement S for *summary* or D for *details*.

_____ a. The girl sways in the darkness, and Heyst feels ashamed.

_____ b. The girl tells Heyst that she never looked at any of the other fellows.

_____ c. Heyst pulls away from the girl and then lies to her about his reason.

Correct Answers, Part A _____

Correct Answers, Part B _____

Total Correct Answers _____

## *from* **The Vanishing American**
### *by Zane Grey*

Morgan's office adjoined the chapel where he preached to the Indians. It was not a severe room by any means. Color and comfort were in evidence. There was an absence of anything of Indian design. This study had two other doors, one opening into the living room, the other out upon a back porch.

Presently Morgan got up and went to the open window. The September morning breeze bore a hint of melting frost. The summer was waning. Already the orchard showed the gold and bronze colors of autumn. But out beyond, the sweep of desert seemed as changeless as it was endless. That wide expanse of green and distance seemed an encompassing barrier. Morgan had no love for the open spaces.

His first visitor that morning was Jay Lord. The Mormon entered without removing sombrero or cigarette, and his bold face wore a mask of a smile. His dusty garb attested to recent travel.

"Howdy, Morgan," he said. "I got back last night. Haven't seen Blucher yet. Reckon I wanted to see you first."

"Did you find out anything?" asked Morgan.

"Wal, yes an' no," returned Lord. "I can't prove what Blucher wants. Them Pahutes are sure closemouthed. But I've a hunch the Carlisle Injun Nophay had a lot to do with Gekin Yashi's disappearance."

"So had I that hunch," retorted the missionary darkly. "Blucher didn't want to send you. He doesn't care now the girl has been brought back. But I care. And I want examples to be made of Do Etin, and whoever rode off with Gekin Yashi."

"Reckon you'll never prove anythin' on either Do Etin, or Nophay," said Lord dryly. "You'll just have to frame them."

"Jay Lord, I don't like your talk."

"Wal, if you don't like it you can lump it," drawled the other. "I told you I was ready to work for your interests, in the dark. An' so I am. But don't call spades hearts to me. I've been ten years' rustlin' round this reservation."

Morgan's pale eyes studied the blunt Mormon, with that somber gaze of a shrewd man who trusted no one.

"Very well. We'll call spades spades," replied Morgan. "I need you. And you want to replace Wolterson. I'll see that Blucher puts the steamroller under him. And I'll pay you besides."

"How much?" asked Lord.

"What it's worth to me," snapped Morgan. "I don't pay men before they work."

**Reading Time** _____

## Recalling Facts

1. Morgan is a
   - ❏ a. miner.
   - ❏ b. missionary.
   - ❏ c. cowboy.

2. The view out of Morgan's window is one of
   - ❏ a. woods.
   - ❏ b. other huts.
   - ❏ c. open spaces.

3. Jay Lord is a
   - ❏ a. Mormon.
   - ❏ b. Indian scout.
   - ❏ c. cattleman.

4. Gekin Yashi is
   - ❏ a. missing.
   - ❏ b. a missionary.
   - ❏ c. a school teacher.

5. Morgan wants to replace
   - ❏ a. Blucher.
   - ❏ b. Do Etin.
   - ❏ c. Wolterson.

## Understanding the Passage

6. Morgan does not appreciate
   - ❏ a. Indian furnishings.
   - ❏ b. the desert landscape.
   - ❏ c. both a and b.

7. Jay Lord has
   - ❏ a. traveled a long way.
   - ❏ b. never seen Morgan before.
   - ❏ c. recently quit smoking.

8. Apparently, Gekin Yashi had
   - ❏ a. not gone away alone.
   - ❏ b. been a missionary.
   - ❏ c. grown tired of desert life.

9. Morgan is
   - ❏ a. trusting.
   - ❏ b. suspicious.
   - ❏ c. generous.

10. Jay Lord can best be described as
    - ❏ a. honest and hardworking.
    - ❏ b. tough and dishonest.
    - ❏ c. someone who has just found religion.

## *from* **The Land of Oz**
### *by L. Frank Baum*

At daybreak Tip was awakened by Jack Pumpkinhead. He rubbed the sleep from his eyes and bathed in a little brook. Then he ate a portion of his bread and cheese. Having thus prepared for a new day the boy said: "Let us start at once. Nine miles is quite a distance. But we ought to reach the Emerald City by noon if no accidents happen."

So the Pumpkinhead was again perched upon the back of the Saw-Horse. The journey was resumed.

The little party had traveled but a short two miles upon their way when the road of yellow brick was parted by a broad and swift river. Tip was puzzled how to cross it. But after a time he discovered a man in a ferryboat approaching from the other side of the stream.

When the man reached the bank Tip asked:

"Will you row us to the other side?"

"Yes, if you have money," returned the ferryman, whose face looked cross and disagreeable.

"But I have no money," said Tip.

"None at all?" inquired the man.

"None at all," answered the boy.

"Then I'll not break my back rowing you over," said the ferryman, decidedly.

"What a nice man!" remarked the Pumpkinhead, smiling.

1. **Recognizing Words in Context**

   Find the word *inquired* in the passage. One definition below is closest to the meaning of that word. One definition has the opposite or nearly the opposite meaning. The remaining definition has a completely different meaning. Label each definition C for *closest*, O for *opposite or nearly opposite*, or D for *different*.

   _____ a. answered

   _____ b. asked

   _____ c. shouted

2. **Keeping Events in Order**

   Number each statement below 1, 2, or 3 to show the order in which the events took place.

   _____ a. Tip and his party come to a river.

   _____ b. The ferryman asks if Tip has money.

   _____ c. Tip bathes in a little brook.

## 3. Making Evaluations

Two of the statements below describe things that actually happen or are stated in the passage. The other statement is an evaluation, or a judgment or opinion, about a character, setting, or event in the passage. Label each statement E for *evaluation* or H for *happens or is stated in the passage.*

_____ a. The ferryman is mean because he doesn't help those who need it.

_____ b. Tip is puzzled about how to cross the river.

_____ c. The ferryman and Tip discuss rowing Tip's party across the river.

## 4. Making Correct Inferences

Two of the statements below are correct inferences, or reasonable guesses. They are based on information in the passage. The other statement is an incorrect, or faulty, inference. Label each statement C for *correct* inference or F for *faulty* inference.

_____ a. Pumpkinhead is not a very good judge of character.

_____ b. Tip must cross the river to reach the Emerald City.

_____ c. The ferryman's boat is not big enough for everyone.

## 5. Summarizing

One of the statements below is a summary that tells the most important ideas in the passage. The other two statements contain details from the passage. They do not tell the most important ideas in the passage. Label each statement S for *summary* or D for *details.*

_____ a. Tip thinks they can reach the Emerald City by noon if no accidents happen.

_____ b. The group must cross a river, but a ferryman refuses to take them.

_____ c. Jack Pumpkinhead rides the Saw-Horse on the trip to the river.

Correct Answers, Part A _____

Correct Answers, Part B _____

Total Correct Answers _____

# *from* **The Custom of the Country**
## *by Edith Wharton*

"Do you mean to tell me that Undine's divorcing me?" Ralph cried.

"I presume that's her plan," Mr. Spragg admitted.

"For desertion?" Ralph pursued, laughing.

His father-in-law hesitated a moment; then he answered: "You've always done all you could for my daughter. There wasn't any other plea she could think of. She presumed this would be the most agreeable to your family."

"It was good of her to think of that!"

Mr. Spragg's only comment was a sigh.

"Does she think I won't fight it?" Ralph broke out with passion.

His father-in-law looked at him thoughtfully. "I presume you realize it ain't easy to change Undine, once she's set on a thing."

"Perhaps not. But if she really means to apply for a divorce I can make it a little less easy for her to get."

"That's so," Mr. Spragg conceded. He turned back to his revolving chair, and seating himself in it began to drum on the desk with cigar-stained fingers.

"And by God, I will!" Ralph thundered. Anger was the only emotion in him now. He had been fooled, cheated, made a mock of; but the score was not settled yet. He turned back and stood before Mr. Spragg. "I suppose she's gone with Van Degen?"

"My daughter's gone alone, sir. I saw her off at the station. I understood she was to join a lady friend."

"Well, does she suppose Van Degen's going to marry her?"

"Undine did not mention her future plans to me." After a moment Mr. Spragg appended: "If she had, I should have declined to discuss them with her."

Ralph looked at him curiously, perceiving that he intended in this negative way to imply his disapproval of his daughter's course.

"I shall fight it! I shall fight it!" the young man cried again. "You may tell her I shall fight it to the end!"

Mr. Spragg pressed the nib of his pen against the dust-coated inkstand. "I suppose you would have to engage a lawyer. She'll know it that way," he remarked.

"She'll know it—you may count on that!"

Ralph began to laugh again. Suddenly he heard his own laugh and it pulled him up. What was he laughing about? What was he talking about? The thing was to act—to hold his tongue and act. There was no use uttering windy threats to this broken-spirited old man.

**Reading Time** _____

## Recalling Facts

1. Ralph hears of Undine's plans for divorce from
   - ❏ a. Mr. Van Degen.
   - ❏ b. his brother-in-law.
   - ❏ c. his father-in-law.

2. Undine is asking for a divorce on the grounds of
   - ❏ a. abuse.
   - ❏ b. desertion.
   - ❏ c. separation.

3. Ralph tells Mr. Spragg he plans to
   - ❏ a. fight the divorce.
   - ❏ b. remarry immediately.
   - ❏ c. confront Undine alone.

4. Undine has gone to join
   - ❏ a. Mr. Spragg.
   - ❏ b. her mother.
   - ❏ c. a lady friend.

5. Mr. Spragg suggests that Ralph
   - ❏ a. get a lawyer.
   - ❏ b. apologize to Undine.
   - ❏ c. go directly to the train station.

## Understanding the Passage

6. When he hears of Undine's plans for divorce, Ralph becomes very
   - ❏ a. quiet.
   - ❏ b. polite.
   - ❏ c. upset.

7. Undine's father does not seem pleased with
   - ❏ a. Undine's behavior.
   - ❏ b. Van Degen's attitude.
   - ❏ c. Ralph's appearance.

8. Undine is apparently a
   - ❏ a. law student.
   - ❏ b. most unattractive woman.
   - ❏ c. stubborn woman.

9. Mr. Spragg believes that Ralph has been
   - ❏ a. good to Undine.
   - ❏ b. a bad influence on Undine.
   - ❏ c. secretly meeting with Van Degen.

10. Ralph suspects Undine
   - ❏ a. is lying to Mr. Spragg.
   - ❏ b. will soon come back to him.
   - ❏ c. wants to marry Van Degen.

*from* **George's Mother**
*by Stephen Crane*

Young Kelcey entered the room. He gave a sigh of relief, and dropped his pail in a corner. He was evidently greatly wearied by a hard day of toil.

The little old woman hobbled over to him and raised her wrinkled lips. She seemed on the verge of tears and an outburst of reproaches.

"Hello!" he cried, in a voice of cheer. "Been gettin' anxious?"

"Yes," she said, hovering about him. "Where yeh been, George? What made yeh so late? I've been waitin' the longest while. Don't throw your coat down there. Hang it up behind the door."

The son put his coat on the proper hook, and then went to splatter water in a tin washbasin at the sink.

"Well, yeh see, I met Jones—you remember Jones? Ol' Handyville fellah. An' we had to stop an' talk over ol' times. Jones is quite a boy."

The little old woman's mouth set in a sudden straight line. "Oh, that Jones," she said. "I don't like him."

The youth interrupted a flurry of white towel to give a glance of irritation. "Well, now, what's the use of talkin' that way?" he said to her. "What do yeh know 'bout 'im? Ever spoke to 'im in yer life?"

1. **Recognizing Words in Context**

   Find the word *irritation* in the passage. One definition below is closest to the meaning of that word. One definition has the opposite or nearly the opposite meaning. The remaining definition has a completely different meaning. Label each definition C for *closest*, O for *opposite or nearly opposite*, or D for *different*.

   _____ a. annoyance

   _____ b. enjoyment

   _____ c. triumph

2. **Keeping Events in Order**

   Number each statement below 1, 2, or 3 to show the order in which the events took place.

   _____ a. George's mother says that she doesn't like Jones.

   _____ b. George asks if his mother ever spoke to Jones.

   _____ c. George talks to Jones about old times.

## 3. Making Evaluations

Two of the statements below describe things that actually happen or are stated in the passage. The other statement is an evaluation, or a judgment or opinion, about a character, setting, or event in the passage. Label each statement E for *evaluation* or H for *happens or is stated in the passage*.

_____ a. George's mother waited a long time for him to return.

_____ b. George speaks disrespectfully to his mother.

_____ c. George's mother seems about to cry.

## 4. Making Correct Inferences

Two of the statements below are correct inferences, or reasonable guesses. They are based on information in the passage. The other statement is an incorrect, or faulty, inference. Label each statement C for *correct* inference or F for *faulty* inference.

_____ a. George's mother is glad to see George but angry that he is late.

_____ b. Jones is a close family friend of George and his mother.

_____ c. George is happy to be home after his long day of work.

## 5. Summarizing

One of the statements below is a summary that tells the most important ideas in the passage. The other two statements contain details from the passage. They do not tell the most important ideas in the passage. Label each statement S for *summary* or D for *details*.

_____ a. George returns home tired and drops his pail in a corner.

_____ b. George's mother explains that she's been waiting for him for a long time.

_____ c. George gets home and has a disagreement with his mother about Jones.

Correct Answers, Part A _____

Correct Answers, Part B _____

Total Correct Answers _____

*from* **The Love Nest**
*by Ring Lardner*

"I'll tell you what I'm going to do with you, Mr. Bartlett," said the great man. "I'm going to take you right out to my home and have you meet the wife and family; stay to dinner and all night. We've got plenty of room and extra pajamas, if you don't mind them silk. I mean that'll give you a chance to see us just as we are. I mean you can get more that way than if you sat here a whole week, asking me questions."

"But I don't want to put you to a lot of trouble," said Bartlett.

"Trouble!" The great man laughed. "There's no trouble about it. I've got a house that's like a hotel. I mean a big house with lots of servants. But anyway I'm always glad to do anything I can for a writing man, especially a man that works for Ralph Doane. I'm very fond of Ralph. I mean I like him personally besides being a great editor. I mean I've known him for years and when there's anything I can do for him, I'm glad to do it. I mean it'll be a pleasure to have you. So if you want to notify your family—"

"I haven't any family," said Bartlett.

"Well, I'm sorry for you! And I bet when you see mine, you'll wish you had one of your own. But I'm glad you can come and we'll start now so as to get there before the kiddies are put away for the night. I mean I want you to be sure and see the kiddies. I've got three."

"I've seen their pictures," said Bartlett. "You must be very proud of them. They're all girls, aren't they?"

"Yes, sir; three girls. I wouldn't have a boy. I mean I always wanted girls. I mean girls have got a lot more zip to them. I mean they're a lot zippier. But let's go! The Rolls is downstairs and if we start now we'll get there before dark. I mean I want you to see the place while it's still daylight."

The great man—Lou Gregg, president of Modern Pictures, Inc.— escorted his visitor from the magnificent office by a private door and down a private stairway to the avenue, where the glittering car with its glittering chauffeur waited.

"My wife was in town today," said Gregg as they glided northward.

**Reading Time** _____

## Recalling Facts

1. The great man's pajamas are made of
   - ❏ a. cotton.
   - ❏ b. silk.
   - ❏ c. wool.

2. The great man compares his house to a
   - ❏ a. lodge.
   - ❏ b. motel.
   - ❏ c. hotel.

3. Mr. Bartlett works for
   - ❏ a. the great man.
   - ❏ b. himself.
   - ❏ c. Ralph Doane.

4. Bartlett
   - ❏ a. has no family.
   - ❏ b. knows the great man well.
   - ❏ c. feels sorry for the great man.

5. The great man is in the
   - ❏ a. movie business.
   - ❏ b. steel industry.
   - ❏ c. used car business.

## Understanding the Passage

6. The great man wants Mr. Bartlett to
   - ❏ a. get to know him personally.
   - ❏ b. conduct long interviews.
   - ❏ c. leave him alone.

7. The great man
   - ❏ a. is having a streak of bad luck.
   - ❏ b. thinks Ralph Doane is a poor boss.
   - ❏ c. is extremely wealthy.

8. The great man especially likes
   - ❏ a. sports stars.
   - ❏ b. writers.
   - ❏ c. photographers.

9. Apparently, the great man
   - ❏ a. wants to have several more children.
   - ❏ b. doesn't think much of boys.
   - ❏ c. wants to keep Mr. Bartlett a prisoner.

10. The great man can best be described as
    - ❏ a. secretive.
    - ❏ b. outgoing and friendly.
    - ❏ c. a happy bachelor.

### *from* **Peter and Wendy**
#### *by James M. Barrie*

Foolish Tootles was standing like a conqueror over Wendy's body when the other boys sprang from their trees. "You are too late," he cried proudly, "I have shot the Wendy. Peter will be so happy."

Overhead Tinker Bell shouted, "You fool!" and darted into hiding. The others did not hear her. They had crowded round Wendy, and as they looked a terrible silence fell. If Wendy's heart had been beating they would all have heard it.

Slightly was the first to speak. "This is no bird," he said in a scared voice. "I think it must be a lady."

"A lady?" said Tootles.

"And we have killed her," Nibs said hoarsely.

They all whipped off their caps.

"Now I see," Curly said; "Peter was bringing her to us." He threw himself sorrowfully on the ground.

"A lady to take care of us at last," said one of the twins, "and you have killed her!"

They were sorry for him, but sorrier for themselves, and when he took a step nearer they turned away. Tootles' face was very white, but there was a dignity to him now that had never been there before.

## 1. Recognizing Words in Context

Find the word *sorrowfully* in the passage. One definition below is closest to the meaning of that word. One definition has the opposite or nearly the opposite meaning. The remaining definition has a completely different meaning. Label each definition C for *closest,* O for *opposite or nearly opposite,* or D for *different.*

_____ a. cheerfully

_____ b. shortly

_____ c. sadly

## 2. Keeping Events in Order

Number each statement below 1, 2, or 3 to show the order in which the events took place.

_____ a. Curly throws himself to the ground in sorrow.

_____ b. Tootles stands like a conqueror over Wendy's body.

_____ c. Slightly says that the body must be a lady.

## 3. Making Evaluations

Two of the statements below describe things that actually happen or are stated in the passage. The other statement is an evaluation, or a judgment or opinion, about a character, setting, or event in the passage. Label each statement E for *evaluation* or H for *happens or is stated in the passage*.

_____ a. Tootles has made a terrible mistake.

_____ b. Tinker Bell calls Tootles a fool.

_____ c. Tootles has a dignity that he never had before.

## 4. Making Correct Inferences

Two of the statements below are correct inferences, or reasonable guesses. They are based on information in the passage. The other statement is an incorrect, or faulty, inference. Label each statement C for *correct* inference or F for *faulty* inference.

_____ a. Tootles wants to please Peter.

_____ b. The boys want to have a lady taking care of them.

_____ c. The boys are very angry with Tootles.

## 5. Summarizing

One of the statements below is a summary that tells the most important ideas in the passage. The other two statements contain details from the passage. They do not tell the most important ideas in the passage. Label each statement S for *summary* or D for *details*.

_____ a. Tootles has shot Wendy, not realizing that Peter brought her.

_____ b. The boys would have heard Wendy's heart if it was beating.

_____ c. The boys all feel sorry for themselves when they realize what they have lost.

Correct Answers, Part A _____

Correct Answers, Part B _____

Total Correct Answers _____

*from* **The Maker of Moons**
*by Robert W. Chambers*

Most old ladies are odd. But there is a limit and my great-aunt had overstepped it. I had believed her to be wealthy; she died bankrupt. Still, I knew there was only one thing she did possess. That was the famous "Crimson Diamond." Now, of course, you know who my great-aunt was.

Excepting the Koh-i-noor, and the Regent, this stone was, as everybody knows, the most valuable gem in the world. Any sane person would have placed that diamond in a safe-deposit box. My great-aunt did nothing of the kind. She kept it in a small velvet bag, which she carried about her neck. She never took it off, but wore it openly on her heavy silk gown.

In this same bag she also carried dried catnip leaves of which she was very fond. Nobody but myself, her only living relative, knew that the Crimson Diamond lay among the sprigs of catnip in the little velvet bag.

"Harold," she would say, "do you think I'm a fool? If I place the gem in any safe-deposit vault in New York, someone would steal it sooner or later." Then she would nibble a sprig of catnip and peer at me. I loathed the odor of catnip and she knew it. I also loathed cats. This also she knew. And, of course, she surrounded herself with a dozen. Poor old lady! On the first day of March, she was found dead in her bed in her apartment at the Waldorf. The doctor said she died from natural causes. The only other occupant of her sleeping room was a cat. The cat fled when we broke open the door, and I heard that she was cherished by some people in a neighboring apartment.

My great-aunt's death was due to purely natural causes. Still, there was one very unpleasant feature of the case. The velvet bag, containing the Crimson Diamond, was gone. Every inch of the apartment was searched. The floors were torn up. The walls were dismantled. But the gem could not be found. Chief of Police Conlin detailed four of his best men to the case, and as I had nothing better to do, I enrolled myself to help out. I also put up a large reward for the recovery of the gem. All New York was agog.

The case seemed hopeless enough, although there were five of us after the thief.

**Reading Time** _____

## Recalling Facts

1. The great-aunt died
   - ❏ a. bankrupt.
   - ❏ b. of unnatural causes.
   - ❏ c. clutching the Crimson Diamond.

2. The great-aunt kept her gem in a
   - ❏ a. safe-deposit vault.
   - ❏ b. small velvet bag.
   - ❏ c. locked closet.

3. The great-aunt loved to nibble on
   - ❏ a. peanuts.
   - ❏ b. catnip.
   - ❏ c. cheese.

4. The narrator hates
   - ❏ a. dogs.
   - ❏ b. snakes.
   - ❏ c. cats.

5. The narrator
   - ❏ a. puts up a reward for the return of the gem.
   - ❏ b. offers to help find the thieves.
   - ❏ c. both a and b.

## Understanding the Passage

6. The "Crimson Diamond" is the
   - ❏ a. most valuable gem in the world.
   - ❏ b. second most valuable gem in the world.
   - ❏ c. third most valuable gem in the world.

7. The great-aunt was apparently
   - ❏ a. well known to many people.
   - ❏ b. warm and friendly to everyone.
   - ❏ c. part of a large family.

8. The narrator thinks that his great-aunt's method for protecting her diamond was
   - ❏ a. brilliant.
   - ❏ b. unoriginal.
   - ❏ c. unsafe.

9. The great-aunt did not trust
   - ❏ a. safe-deposit vaults.
   - ❏ b. the narrator.
   - ❏ c. both a and b.

10. The police consider the case of the missing gem
    - ❏ a. impossible to solve.
    - ❏ b. not worth much effort.
    - ❏ c. extremely important.

# *from* Tess of the d'Urbervilles
## *by Thomas Hardy*

Ever since the accident with her father's horse, Tess, courageous as she naturally was, had been exceedingly timid on wheels. She began to get uneasy at a certain recklessness in her conductor's driving.

"You will go down slow, sir, I suppose?" she said.

D'Urberville looked round upon her, nipped his cigar with the tips of his large white center teeth, and allowed his lips to smile slowly.

"Why, Tess," he answered, after another whiff or two, "it isn't a brave bouncing girl like you who asks that? Why, I always go down at full gallop. There's nothing like it for raising your spirits."

"But perhaps you need not now?"

"Ah," he said, shaking his head, "there are two to be reckoned with. It is not me alone. Tib has to be considered, and she has a very queer temper."

"Who?"

"Why, this mare. I fancy she looked round at me in a very grim way just then. Didn't you notice it?"

"Don't try to frighten me, sir," said Tess stiffly.

"Well, I don't. If any living man can manage this horse I can:—I won't say any living man can do it—but if such has the power, I am he."

1. **Recognizing Words in Context**

   Find the word *timid* in the passage. One definition below is closest to the meaning of that word. One definition has the opposite or nearly the opposite meaning. The remaining definition has a completely different meaning. Label each definition C for *closest,* O for *opposite or nearly opposite,* or D for *different.*

   _____ a. fearful

   _____ b. brave

   _____ c. intelligent

2. **Keeping Events in Order**

   Number each statement below 1, 2, or 3 to show the order in which the events took place.

   _____ a. An accident takes place with Tess's father's horse.

   _____ b. D'Urberville tells Tess that he can manage the horse.

   _____ c. Tess asks d'Urberville if he will go down the hill slowly.

## 3. Making Evaluations

Two of the statements below describe things that actually happen or are stated in the passage. The other statement is an evaluation, or a judgment or opinion, about a character, setting, or event in the passage. Label each statement E for *evaluation* or H for *happens or is stated in the passage*.

_____ a. Tess feels uneasy about her conductor's driving.

_____ b. D'Urberville tells Tess that the mare looked at him.

_____ c. D'Urberville is overly confident in his driving ability.

## 4. Making Correct Inferences

Two of the statements below are correct inferences, or reasonable guesses. They are based on information in the passage. The other statement is an incorrect, or faulty, inference. Label each statement C for *correct* inference or F for *faulty* inference.

_____ a. D'Urberville needs to drive fast because they are late.

_____ b. It is not like Tess to be so easily frightened.

_____ c. D'Urberville is not a cautious driver.

## 5. Summarizing

One of the statements below is a summary that tells the most important ideas in the passage. The other two statements contain details from the passage. They do not tell the most important ideas in the passage. Label each statement S for *summary* or D for *details*.

_____ a. After an accident with her father's horse, Tess has become timid.

_____ b. Tess is uneasy on wheels, but d'Urberville refuses to go slowly.

_____ c. D'Urberville says that the horse has a queer temper.

Correct Answers, Part A _____

Correct Answers, Part B _____

Total Correct Answers _____

### *from* **The Water of Life**
#### *by The Brothers Grimm*

There was once a King who had an illness. No one believed that he would come out of it with his life. He had three sons who were much distressed about it. They went down into the palace garden and wept. There they met an old man who inquired as to the cause of their grief. They told him that their father was so ill that he would most certainly die, for nothing seemed to cure him. Then the old man said, "I know of one more remedy. It is the water of life. If he drinks it he will become well again. But it is hard to find." The eldest said, "I will manage to find it." He went to the sick King and begged to be allowed to go forth in search of the water of life. "No," said the King, "it is too dangerous. I would rather die." But he begged so long that the King consented. The prince thought in his heart, "If I bring the water, then I shall be best beloved of my father, and shall inherit the kingdom." So he set out. Soon he met a dwarf in the road who called to him, saying, "Where are you going so fast?" "Silly shrimp," said the prince, very haughtily, "it is nothing to you," and rode on. But the little dwarf had grown angry. He had wished an evil wish. Presently the prince entered a ravine. The further he rode, the closer the mountains drew together. At last the road became so narrow that he could not advance a step further. It was impossible either to turn his horse or to dismount, and he was shut in there as if in prison. The sick King waited long for him, but he came not. The second son said, "Father, let me go forth to seek the water," and thought, "If my brother is dead, then the kingdom will fall to me." At first the King would not allow him to go either. At last, though, he yielded. The prince set out on the same road that his brother had taken. He too met the dwarf, who stopped him to ask where he was going in such haste? "Little shrimp," said the prince, "that is nothing to you," and rode on without giving him another look. But the dwarf bewitched him, and he, like the other, got caught in a ravine.

## Recalling Facts

1. The King has
   - ❏ a. one son.
   - ❏ b. two sons.
   - ❏ c. three sons.

2. The old man in the garden says he
   - ❏ a. knows of a remedy.
   - ❏ b. will prepare a remedy.
   - ❏ c. has misplaced a known remedy.

3. The "silly shrimp" refers to a
   - ❏ a. frog.
   - ❏ b. grasshopper.
   - ❏ c. dwarf.

4. The princes become trapped in a
   - ❏ a. ravine.
   - ❏ b. cave.
   - ❏ c. dungeon.

5. The eldest son travels by
   - ❏ a. boat.
   - ❏ b. horse.
   - ❏ c. foot.

## Understanding the Passage

6. Apparently, the doctors in the kingdom
   - ❏ a. don't know how sick the King is.
   - ❏ b. can't cure the King.
   - ❏ c. know about the water of life.

7. The water of life
   - ❏ a. can be found only on the palace grounds.
   - ❏ b. is hard to locate.
   - ❏ c. cures only kings and nobles.

8. When the eldest son asks if he can look for the water of life, the King
   - ❏ a. finally agrees.
   - ❏ b. cannot make up his mind.
   - ❏ c. persistently refuses.

9. Both princes want to
   - ❏ a. save their father's life.
   - ❏ b. inherit the kingdom.
   - ❏ c. both a and b.

10. The dwarf has
    - ❏ a. no friends.
    - ❏ b. magical powers.
    - ❏ c. advice for searchers.

## 11　B　*from* **One Crowded Hour**
### *by Arthur Conan Doyle*

Still the young man did not speak. He was clearly on the edge of an interview which he found most difficult to open. His host grew impatient.

"You don't seem yourself this morning. What on earth is the matter? Anything upset you?"

"Yes," said Ronald Barker, with emphasis. "You have upset me."

Sir Henry smiled. "Sit down, my dear fellow. If you have any grievance against me, let me hear it."

Barker sat down. He seemed to be gathering himself for a reproach. When it did come it was like a bullet from a gun.

"Why did you rob me last night?"

The magistrate was a man of iron nerve. He showed neither surprise nor resentment. Not a muscle moved upon his calm, set face.

"Why do you say that I robbed you last night?"

"A big, tall fellow in a motorcar stopped me on the Mayfield road. He poked a pistol in my face and took my purse and my watch. Sir Henry, that man was you."

The magistrate smiled. "Am I the only big, tall man in the district? Am I the only man with a motorcar?"

"Do you think I couldn't tell a Rolls Royce when I see it—I, who spend half my life on a car and the other half under it? Who has a Rolls Royce about here except you?"

### 1. Recognizing Words in Context

Find the word *grievance* in the passage. One definition below is closest to the meaning of that word. One definition has the opposite or nearly the opposite meaning. The remaining definition has a completely different meaning. Label each definition C for *closest,* O for *opposite or nearly opposite,* or D for *different.*

_____ a. result

_____ b. praise

_____ c. complaint

### 2. Keeping Events in Order

Number each statement below 1, 2, or 3 to show the order in which the events took place.

_____ a. Ronald Barker accuses Sir Henry of robbing him.

_____ b. Sir Henry invites Ronald Barker to sit down.

_____ c. Sir Henry grows impatient with Ronald Barker's silence.

## 3. Making Evaluations

Two of the statements below describe things that actually happen or are stated in the passage. The other statement is an evaluation, or a judgment or opinion, about a character, setting, or event in the passage. Label each statement E for *evaluation* or H for *happens or is stated in the passage*.

_____ a. Sir Henry has upset Ronald Barker.

_____ b. Sir Henry owns a Rolls Royce.

_____ c. Sir Henry is a cold, calculating man.

## 4. Making Correct Inferences

Two of the statements below are correct inferences, or reasonable guesses. They are based on information in the passage. The other statement is an incorrect, or faulty, inference. Label each statement C for *correct* inference or F for *faulty* inference.

_____ a. Ronald Barker feels uncomfortable accusing Sir Henry.

_____ b. Sir Henry is a wealthy man.

_____ c. Sir Henry became rich by robbing people.

## 5. Summarizing

One of the statements below is a summary that tells the most important ideas in the passage. The other two statements contain details from the passage. They do not tell the most important ideas in the passage. Label each statement S for *summary* or D for *details*.

_____ a. Ronald Barker is robbed one night and accuses Sir Henry of the crime.

_____ b. Sir Henry becomes impatient with Ronald Barker when he fails to speak.

_____ c. A fellow poked a pistol in Ronald Barker's face and took his purse.

Correct Answers, Part A _____

Correct Answers, Part B _____

Total Correct Answers _____

*from* **The Picture of Dorian Gray**
*by Oscar Wilde*

James walked up and down the room two or three times. Then he turned to the still figure in the chair. "Mother, are my things ready?" he asked.

"Quite ready, James," she answered, keeping her eyes on her work. For some months past she had felt ill at ease when she was alone with this rough, stern son of hers. Her shallow nature was troubled when their eyes met. She began to complain. Women defend themselves by attacking, just as they attack by sudden and strange surrenders. "I hope you will be contented, James, with your sea-faring life," she said. "You must remember that it is your own choice. You might have entered a solicitor's office. Solicitors are a very respectable class. In the country they often dine with the best families."

"I hate offices, and I hate clerks," he replied. "But you are quite right. I have chosen my own life. All I say is, watch over my sister. Don't let her come to any harm. Mother, you must watch over her."

"James, you really talk very strangely. Of course I watch over Sibyl."

"I hear a gentleman comes every night to the theater, and goes behind to talk to her. Is that right? What about that?"

"You are speaking about things you don't understand, James. In the acting profession we are accustomed to receive a great deal of attention. I myself used to receive many bouquets at one time. That was when acting was really understood. As for Sibyl, I do not know at present whether her attachment is serious or not. But there is no doubt that the young man in question is a perfect gentleman. He is always most polite to me. Besides, he has the appearance of being rich, and the flowers he sends are lovely."

"You don't know his name, though," said the lad, harshly.

"No," answered his mother, with a placid expression in her face. "He has not yet revealed his real name. I think it is quite romantic of him. He is probably a member of the aristocracy."

James Vane bit his lip. "Watch over Sibyl, mother," he cried, "watch over her."

"My son, you distress me very much. Sibyl is always under my special care. Of course, if this gentleman is wealthy, there is no reason why she could not contract an alliance with him. I trust he is one of the aristocracy."

**Reading Time** _____

## Recalling Facts

1. When alone with her son, the mother feels
   - ❑ a. sad.
   - ❑ b. uncomfortable.
   - ❑ c. content.

2. The mother considers solicitors to be
   - ❑ a. members of the lower class.
   - ❑ b. untrustworthy.
   - ❑ c. very respectable.

3. James hates
   - ❑ a. his sister.
   - ❑ b. clerks.
   - ❑ c. actors.

4. The gentleman who is seeing Sibyl is
   - ❑ a. polite.
   - ❑ b. trustworthy.
   - ❑ c. rude.

5. James asks his mother to
   - ❑ a. watch over Sibyl.
   - ❑ b. take care of herself.
   - ❑ c. work in the theater.

## Understanding the Passage

6. James apparently does not
   - ❑ a. trust his mother.
   - ❑ b. want to leave home.
   - ❑ c. like theater people.

7. James is heading off to
   - ❑ a. law school.
   - ❑ b. sea.
   - ❑ c. the stage.

8. The gentleman is keeping
   - ❑ a. Sibyl from leaving the theater.
   - ❑ b. a promise to his grandmother.
   - ❑ c. at least one secret from Sibyl and her mother.

9. The mother believes she is
   - ❑ a. taking good care of her daughter.
   - ❑ b. responsible for her husband's death.
   - ❑ c. going to marry the wealthy gentleman.

10. James apparently thinks his sister is
   - ❑ a. a bad actress.
   - ❑ b. in some danger.
   - ❑ c. smarter than he is.

## 12  B  *from* **The Virginian**
### *by Owen Wister*

"Didn't I tell you he'd not shoot?" the dealer said. "You got ready to dodge. You had no call to be concerned. He's not the kind a man need feel anxious about."

The player looked over at the Virginian, doubtfully. "Well," he said, "I don't know what you folks call a dangerous man."

"Not him!" exclaimed the dealer. "He's a brave man. That's different."

The player seemed to follow this reasoning no better than I did.

"It's not a brave man that's dangerous," continued the dealer. "It's the cowards that scare me." He paused that this might sink home. "Fellow came in here last Tuesday," he went on. "He got into some misunderstanding about the drinks. Well, sir, before we could put him out of business, he'd hurt two perfectly innocent onlookers. They'd no more to do with it than you have," the dealer said to me.

"Were they badly hurt?" I asked.

"One of 'em was. He's died since."

"What became of the man?"

"Why, we put him out of business, I told you. He died that night. But there was no occasion for any of it; and that's why I never like to be around where there's a coward."

## 1. Recognizing Words in Context

Find the word *anxious* in the passage. One definition below is closest to the meaning of that word. One definition has the opposite or nearly the opposite meaning. The remaining definition has a completely different meaning. Label each definition C for *closest*, O for *opposite or nearly opposite,* or D for *different*.

_____ a. worried

_____ b. friendly

_____ c. calm

## 2. Keeping Events in Order

Number each statement below 1, 2, or 3 to show the order in which the events took place.

_____ a. A man gets into a misunderstanding about drinks.

_____ b. The dealer tells the player that cowards scare him.

_____ c. Two innocent onlookers are injured.

## 3. Making Evaluations

Two of the statements below describe things that actually happen or are stated in the passage. The other statement is an evaluation, or a judgment or opinion, about a character, setting, or event in the passage. Label each statement E for *evaluation* or H for *happens or is stated in the passage*.

_____ a. The dealer is scared by cowards.

_____ b. The dealer is a good storyteller.

_____ c. The dealer calls the Virginian a brave man.

## 4. Making Correct Inferences

Two of the statements below are correct inferences, or reasonable guesses. They are based on information in the passage. The other statement is an incorrect, or faulty, inference. Label each statement C for *correct* inference or F for *faulty* inference.

_____ a. The dealer put the Virginian out of business.

_____ b. The dealer feels respect for the Virginian.

_____ c. The player feels the Virginian might be dangerous.

## 5. Summarizing

One of the statements below is a summary that tells the most important ideas in the passage. The other two statements contain details from the passage. They do not tell the most important ideas in the passage. Label each statement S for *summary* or D for *details*.

_____ a. The dealer tells the player the Virginian would not shoot.

_____ b. The dealer explains the difference between brave people and dangerous people.

_____ c. A man gets into a misunderstanding about drinks.

Correct Answers, Part A _____

Correct Answers, Part B _____

Total Correct Answers _____

*from* **Tom Sawyer Abroad**
*by Mark Twain*

We went to sleep about four o'clock, and woke up about eight. The professor was setting back there at his end, looking glum. He pitched us some breakfast, but he told us not to come abaft the midship compass. That was about the middle of the boat. Well, when you are sharp-set, and you eat and satisfy yourself, everything looks pretty different from what it done before. It makes a body feel pretty comfortable, even when he is up in a balloon with a genius. We got to talking together. There was one thing that kept bothering me, and by and by I says: "Tom, didn't we start east?"

"Yes."

"How fast have we been going?"

"Well, you heard what the professor said when he was raging round. Sometimes, he said, we was making fifty miles an hour, sometimes ninety, sometimes a hundred; said with a gale he could go three hundred any time and said if he wanted a gale, and wanted it blowing the right way, he only had to go higher or lower to find it."

"Well, then, it's just as I reckoned. The professor lied."

"Why? What makes you think he lied?"

"If we was going so fast we'd be past Illinois, wouldn't we?"

"Certainly."

"Well, we ain't."

"What's the reason we ain't?"

"I know by the color. We're right over Illinois yet, and you can see for yourself that Indiana ain't in sight."

"I wonder what's the matter with you, Huck. You know by the *color*? Have you lost your mind? What's the color got to do with it?"

"It's got everything to do with it. Illinois is green; Indiana is pink. You can't show me any pink down there. It's all green."

"Indiana *pink*? Why, what a lie!"

"It ain't no lie; I've seen it on the map, and it's pink."

You never see a person so aggravated and disgusted. He says: "Well, if I was such a numbskull as you, Huck Finn, I would jump over. Seen it on the map! Huck Finn, did you reckon the states was the same color out-of-doors as they are on the map?"

"Tom Sawyer, what's a map for? Ain't it to learn you the facts?"

"Of course."

"Well, then, how's it going to do that if it tells lies? That's what I want to know."

"Shucks, you muggins! It don't tell lies."

**Reading Time** _____

**Recalling Facts**

1. At eight o'clock, the professor is looking
   - ❏ a. happy.
   - ❏ b. surprised.
   - ❏ c. glum.

2. The professor says that in a gale the balloon can make
   - ❏ a. 25 miles per hour.
   - ❏ b. 50 miles per hour.
   - ❏ c. 300 miles per hour.

3. Huck says that Indiana should be
   - ❏ a. green.
   - ❏ b. pink.
   - ❏ c. blue.

4. Huck believes
   - ❏ a. what the professor says.
   - ❏ b. that Tom knows where Indiana is.
   - ❏ c. the maps he has seen.

5. Tom thinks Huck is
   - ❏ a. a numbskull.
   - ❏ b. a genius.
   - ❏ c. color-blind.

**Understanding the Passage**

6. Tom is not sure
   - ❏ a. exactly how fast they are going.
   - ❏ b. if Huck is joking or not.
   - ❏ c. both a and b.

7. The person in charge of the journey is
   - ❏ a. Tom.
   - ❏ b. Huck.
   - ❏ c. the professor.

8. The professor appears to be
   - ❏ a. rather moody.
   - ❏ b. extremely cruel.
   - ❏ c. afraid of adventure.

9. Huck is convinced that the professor
   - ❏ a. wants to harm them.
   - ❏ b. is not telling the truth.
   - ❏ c. is not really a professor.

10. Huck believes that maps
    - ❏ a. are often wrong.
    - ❏ b. never lie.
    - ❏ c. are very hard to read.

## 13 | B | *from* **Little Men**

### *by Louisa May Alcott*

"I like a fiddle best; I can play one too," said Nat, getting confidential on this attractive subject.

"Can you?" and Tommy stared over the rim of his mug with round eyes, full of interest. "Mr. Bhaer's got an old fiddle, and he'll let you play on it if you want to."

"Could I? Oh, I would like it ever so much. You see I used to go round fiddling with my father, and another man, till he died."

"Wasn't that fun?" cried Tommy, much impressed.

"No, it was horrid, so cold in winter, and hot in summer. And I got tired, and they were cross sometimes, and I didn't have enough to eat." Nat paused to take a bite of gingerbread, as if to assure himself that the hard times were over, and then he added regretfully, "But I did love my little fiddle, and I miss it. Nicolo took it away when father died, and wouldn't have me any longer, 'cause I was sick."

"You'll belong to the band if you play good. See if you don't."

"Do you have a band here?" And Nat's eyes sparkled.

"Guess we do, a jolly band, all boys, and they have concerts and things."

## 1. Recognizing Words in Context

Find the word *attractive* in the passage. One definition below is closest to the meaning of that word. One definition has the opposite or nearly the opposite meaning. The remaining definition has a completely different meaning. Label each definition C for *closest*, O for *opposite or nearly opposite*, or D for *different*.

_____ a. unwelcome

_____ b. pleasing

_____ c. beautiful

## 2. Keeping Events in Order

Number each statement below 1, 2, or 3 to show the order in which the events took place.

_____ a. Nat tells Tommy that he plays the fiddle.

_____ b. Tommy tells Nat that he can play in the boys' band.

_____ c. Nicolo takes away Nat's fiddle.

## 3. Making Evaluations

Two of the statements below describe things that actually happen or are stated in the passage. The other statement is an evaluation, or a judgment or opinion, about a character, setting, or event in the passage. Label each statement E for *evaluation* or H for *happens or is stated in the passage*.

_____ a. Nat tells Tommy about his past.

_____ b. Nat misses his fiddle.

_____ c. Tommy is very enthusiastic about music.

## 4. Making Correct Inferences

Two of the statements below are correct inferences, or reasonable guesses. They are based on information in the passage. The other statement is an incorrect, or faulty, inference. Label each statement C for *correct* inference or F for *faulty* inference.

_____ a. Nat traveled a great deal as a young child.

_____ b. Tommy has not experienced hardship the way that Nat has.

_____ c. Tommy is a member of the boys' band.

## 5. Summarizing

One of the statements below is a summary that tells the most important ideas in the passage. The other two statements contain details from the passage. They do not tell the most important ideas in the passage. Label each statement S for *summary* or D for *details*.

_____ a. Mr. Bhaer has an old fiddle, and he will let Nat play it.

_____ b. Nat had a difficult childhood.

_____ c. When Tommy learns Nat fiddles, he tells him about a boys' band.

Correct Answers, Part A _____

Correct Answers, Part B _____

Total Correct Answers _____

## 14  A    *from* **White Fang**
### *by Jack London*

"This be the sign of it," Gray Beaver went on. "It is plain that his mother is Kiche. But his father was a wolf. Wherefore is there in him little dog and much wolf. His fangs be white, and White Fang shall be his name. I have spoken. He is my dog. For was not Kiche my brother's dog? And is not my brother dead?"

The cub, who had thus received a name in the world, lay and watched. For a time the man-animals continued to make their mouth-noises. Then Gray Beaver took a knife from the sheath that hung around his neck, and went into the thicket and cut a stick. White Fang watched him. He notched the stick at each end and in the notches fastened strings of raw hide. One string he tied around the throat of Kiche. Then he led her to a small pine, around which he tied the other string.

White Fang followed and lay down beside her. Salmon Tongue's hand reached out to him and rolled him over on his back. Kiche looked on anxiously. White Fang felt fear mounting in him again. He could not quite suppress a snarl, but he made no offer to snap. The hand, with fingers crooked and spread apart, rubbed his stomach in a playful way and rolled him from side to side. It was ridiculous and ungainly, lying there on his back with legs sprawling in the air. Besides, it was a position of such utter helplessness that White Fang's whole nature revolted against it. He could do nothing to defend himself. If this man-animal intended harm, White Fang knew that he could not escape it. How could he spring away with his four legs in the air above him? Yet submission made him master his fear, and he only growled softly. This growl he could not suppress; nor did the man-animal resent it by giving him a blow on the head. And furthermore, such was the strangeness of it, White Fang experienced a sensation of pleasure as the hand rubbed back and forth. When he was rolled on his side he ceased the growl; when the fingers pressed and prodded at the base of his ears the pleasurable sensation increased; and when, with a final rub and scratch, the man left him alone and went away, all fear had died out of White Fang.

**Reading Time** _____

## Recalling Facts

1. White Fang's mother is
   ❏ a. Gray Beaver.
   ❏ b. Kiche.
   ❏ c. a wolf.

2. White Fang
   ❏ a. belongs to Gray Beaver.
   ❏ b. is a full-blooded wolf.
   ❏ c. was abandoned by his pack.

3. Gray Beaver uses his knife to cut a
   ❏ a. piece of rope.
   ❏ b. stick.
   ❏ c. notch in a tree.

4. Salmon Tongue
   ❏ a. clubs White Fang.
   ❏ b. names his dog White Fang.
   ❏ c. rubs White Fang's stomach.

5. White Fang's nature revolts against
   ❏ a. lying with his legs in the air.
   ❏ b. growling at a human being.
   ❏ c. feeling pleasure from the
       man's hand.

## Understanding the Passage

6. Gray Beaver claims White Fang because
   ❏ a. he found him.
   ❏ b. he named the dog.
   ❏ c. his dead brother once owned
       Kiche.

7. Mouth-noises are made by
   ❏ a. wolves.
   ❏ b. humans.
   ❏ c. dogs.

8. White Fang has
   ❏ a. never been played with by a
       human before.
   ❏ b. no feelings for Kiche.
   ❏ c. been tied to a tree many times.

9. White Fang does not like lying on his back because
   ❏ a. the position is painful.
   ❏ b. he feels powerless.
   ❏ c. he cannot growl.

10. Eventually, White Fang discovers that Salmon Tongue
    ❏ a. is an enemy.
    ❏ b. wants to destroy his spirit.
    ❏ c. is friendly.

# *from* **The Exiles**
### *by Richard Harding Davis*

A few hours later Carroll was watching the roulette wheel in the gambling hall of the Isabella when he saw Meakim come in out of the darkness and stand staring in the doorway, blinking at the lights and mopping his face. He had been running, and was visibly excited. Carroll crossed over to him and pushed him out into the quiet of the terrace. "What is it?" he asked.

"Have you seen Holcombe?" Meakim demanded in reply.

"Not since this afternoon. Why?"

Meakim breathed heavily, and fanned himself with his hat. "Well, he's after Winthrop Allen, that's all," he panted. "And when he finds him there's going to be a muss. The boy's gone crazy. He's not safe."

"Why? What do you mean? What's Allen done to him?"

"Nothing to him, but to a friend of his. He got a letter tonight in the mail that came with Allen. It was from his sister. She wrote him all the latest news about Allen, and give him fits for robbing an old lady who'd been kind to her. She wanted that Holcombe should come right back and see what could be done about it. She didn't know, of course, that Allen was coming here. The old lady kept a private school on Fifth Avenue, and Allen had charge of her savings."

## 1. Recognizing Words in Context

Find the word *muss* in the passage. One definition below is closest to the meaning of that word. One definition has the opposite or nearly the opposite meaning. The remaining definition has a completely different meaning. Label each definition C for *closest*, O for *opposite or nearly opposite*, or D for *different*.

_____ a. fight

_____ b. parade

_____ c. compromise

## 2. Keeping Events in Order

Number each statement below 1, 2, or 3 to show the order in which the events took place.

_____ a. Holcombe's sister writes him a letter.

_____ b. Meakim stands in the doorway of the Isabella.

_____ c. Meakim tells Carroll that Holcombe has gone crazy.

## 3. Making Evaluations

Two of the statements below describe things that actually happen or are stated in the passage. The other statement is an evaluation, or a judgment or opinion, about a character, setting, or event in the passage. Label each statement E for *evaluation* or H for *happens or is stated in the passage*.

_____ a. Meakim is breathing heavily.

_____ b. Holcombe is somewhat hotheaded.

_____ c. Holcombe's sister has accused Allen of robbery.

## 4. Making Correct Inferences

Two of the statements below are correct inferences, or reasonable guesses. They are based on information in the passage. The other statement is an incorrect, or faulty, inference. Label each statement C for *correct* inference or F for *faulty* inference.

_____ a. Carroll knows what Holcombe looks like.

_____ b. Meakim helped Allen rob the old lady.

_____ c. Holcombe is protective of his sister.

## 5. Summarizing

One of the statements below is a summary that tells the most important ideas in the passage. The other two statements contain details from the passage. They do not tell the most important ideas in the passage. Label each statement S for *summary* or D for *details*.

_____ a. Carroll sees Meakim blinking at the lights and mopping his face.

_____ b. Meakim tells Carroll that Holcombe means to do Winthrop Allen harm.

_____ c. Holcombe receives a letter from his sister about Winthrop Allen.

Correct Answers, Part A _____

Correct Answers, Part B _____

Total Correct Answers _____

"Where is my husband?" the lady shouted. "I don't care whether he is here or not. But I ought to tell you that the money has been missed, and they are looking for Nikolay Petrovitch. They mean to arrest him. That's your doing!"

The lady got up and walked about the room in great excitement. Pasha looked at her and was so frightened that she couldn't understand.

"He'll be found and arrested today," said the lady, and she gave a sob, and in that sound could be heard her resentment. "I know who has brought him to this awful position! You low, horrid creature! Loathsome, mercenary hussy!"

The lady's lips worked and her nose wrinkled up with disgust. "I am helpless, do you hear, you low woman? I am helpless; you are stronger than I am, but there is One to defend me and my children! God sees all! He is just! He will punish you for every tear I have shed, for all my sleepless nights! The time will come; you will think of me!"

Silence followed again. Pasha gazed blankly at the lady in amazement, not understanding and expecting something awful.

"I know nothing about it, madam," she said, and then burst into tears.

"You are lying!" cried the lady, and her eyes flashed angrily at her. "I know all about it! I've known you a long time. I know that for the last month he has been spending every day with you!"

"Yes. What then? What of it? I have a great many visitors, but I don't force anyone to come. He is free to do as he likes."

"I tell you they have learned that money is missing! He has embezzled money at the office! For the sake of such a creature as you, for your sake he has actually committed a crime. Listen," said the lady in a firm voice, stopping short, facing Pasha, "you can have no principles; you live simply to do harm—that's your goal; but one can't imagine you have fallen so low that you have no trace of human feeling left! He has a wife, children. If he is condemned and sent into exile we shall starve, the children and I. Understand that! And yet there is a chance of saving him and us from poverty and disgrace. If I take them nine hundred rubles today they will let him alone."

**Reading Time** _____

## Recalling Facts

1. The lady says that the
   - ❏ a. money has been missed.
   - ❏ b. police are with her.
   - ❏ c. stolen funds have been returned.

2. The lady says that Nikolay Petrovitch will be
   - ❏ a. shot.
   - ❏ b. beaten.
   - ❏ c. arrested.

3. The lady blames
   - ❏ a. herself.
   - ❏ b. Pasha.
   - ❏ c. God.

4. Pasha says that she has
   - ❏ a. a great deal of money.
   - ❏ b. many visitors.
   - ❏ c. known Nikolay for years.

5. Nikolay
   - ❏ a. is innocent.
   - ❏ b. has children.
   - ❏ c. faces starvation.

## Understanding the Passage

6. The lady appears to be most concerned about her husband's
   - ❏ a. physical health.
   - ❏ b. business connections.
   - ❏ c. ability to support his family.

7. Apparently, the police
   - ❏ a. suspect Nikolay.
   - ❏ b. have no suspects.
   - ❏ c. are unaware of any crime.

8. The lady can best be described as
   - ❏ a. bitter.
   - ❏ b. resigned.
   - ❏ c. hopeful.

9. The lady strongly believes in
   - ❏ a. personal freedom.
   - ❏ b. divine justice.
   - ❏ c. the power of forgiveness.

10. According to the lady, there is
    - ❏ a. no hope for Nikolay.
    - ❏ b. a way out of the situation.
    - ❏ c. no reason to be worried.

## 15　B　　*from* **It's Perfectly True!**

### *by Hans Christian Andersen*

It happened in a henhouse at the other end of the town. The sun went down and the hens flew up. One of them was a white-feathered, short-legged, nice little thing who laid her eggs regularly—a most respectable hen in every way. She settled herself on the perch, preening herself with her beak. One tiny feather fluttered down.

"There's that feather gone!" said the hen. "Well, well, the more I preen myself, the more handsome I shall become, no doubt!"

She said it only in fun, you know. She was the life and soul of that crowd, but otherwise, as we've said, most respectable. Then she fell asleep.

All was dark. There sat the hens, packed closely together. But the white hen's neighbor wasn't asleep; she had heard and not heard, as one must do in this world for the sake of peace and quiet. But she couldn't resist telling it to her neighbor on the other side.

"Did you hear? Well, my dear, I won't mention names, but there's one hen I know who is going to pluck out all her feathers just to make herself look smart. Humph! If I were a rooster I should simply treat her with contempt."

1. **Recognizing Words in Context**

   Find the word *contempt* in the passage. One definition below is closest to the meaning of that word. One definition has the opposite or nearly the opposite meaning. The remaining definition has a completely different meaning. Label each definition C for *closest*, O for *opposite or nearly opposite*, or D for *different*.

   _____ a. sadness

   _____ b. admiration

   _____ c. scorn

2. **Keeping Events in Order**

   Number each statement below 1, 2, or 3 to show the order in which the events took place.

   _____ a. The white hen falls asleep.

   _____ b. One feather falls out as the white hen preens.

   _____ c. The white hen's neighbor speaks to her neighbor on the other side.

## 3. Making Evaluations

Two of the statements below describe things that actually happen or are stated in the passage. The other statement is an evaluation, or a judgment or opinion, about a character, setting, or event in the passage. Label each statement E for *evaluation* or H for *happens or is stated in the passage.*

_____ a. The white hen's neighbor is wrong to spread rumors.

_____ b. The white hen is the life and soul of the crowd.

_____ c. The white hen's neighbor overhears what the white hen says.

## 4. Making Correct Inferences

Two of the statements below are correct inferences, or reasonable guesses. They are based on information in the passage. The other statement is an incorrect, or faulty, inference. Label each statement C for *correct* inference or F for *faulty* inference.

_____ a. The white hen's neighbor is not good at keeping secrets.

_____ b. The white hen is happy and lighthearted.

_____ c. The white hen wants to be more beautiful than the other hens.

## 5. Summarizing

One of the statements below is a summary that tells the most important ideas in the passage. The other two statements contain details from the passage. They do not tell the most important ideas in the passage. Label each statement S for *summary* or D for *details*.

_____ a. As the white hen preens herself, one feather flutters to the ground.

_____ b. The white hen lays her eggs on time and is respectable in every way.

_____ c. The neighbor hen starts a rumor based on something the white hen said.

Correct Answers, Part A _____

Correct Answers, Part B _____

Total Correct Answers _____

*from* **The Adventures of Tom Sawyer**
*by Mark Twain*

Joe's spirits had gone down almost beyond resurrection. He was so homesick that he could hardly endure the misery of it. The tears lay very near the surface. Huck was melancholy, too. Tom was downhearted, but tried hard not to show it. He had a secret which he was not ready to tell, yet, but if this mutinous depression was not broken up soon, he would have to bring it out. He said, with a great show of cheerfulness:

"I bet there's been pirates on this island before, boys. We'll explore it again; they've hid treasures here somewhere. How'd you feel to light on a rotten chest full of gold and silver—hey?"

But it roused only a faint enthusiasm, which faded out, with no reply. Tom tried one or two other seductions; but they failed, too. It was discouraging work. Joe sat poking up the sand with a stick and looking very gloomy. Finally he said:

"Oh, boys, let's give it up; I want to go home."

"Oh, no, Joe, you'll feel better by and by," said Tom; "and just think of the fishing that's here."

"I don't care for fishing; I want to go home."

"But, Joe, there ain't such another swimming place anywhere."

"Swimming's no good. I don't seem to care for it, somehow, when there ain't anybody to say I shan't go in. I mean to go home."

"Baby! You want to see your mother, I reckon."

"Yes, I *do* want to see my mother—and you would, too, if you had one. I ain't any more baby than you are." And Joe snuffled a little.

"Well, we'll let the crybaby go home to his mother, *won't* we Huck? Poor thing—does it want to see its mother? And so it shall. You like it here, don't you, Huck?"

Huck said, "Y-e-s"—without any heart in it.

"I'll never speak to you again as long as I live," said Joe, rising. "There now!" And he moved moodily away and began to dress himself.

"Who cares!" said Tom; "nobody wants you to. Go along home and get laughed at. Oh, you're a nice pirate. Huck and me ain't crybabies; we'll stay, won't we, Huck? Let him go if he wants to. I reckon we can get along without him, perhaps."

But Tom was uneasy, nevertheless, and was alarmed to see Joe go sullenly on with his dressing.

**Reading Time** _____

## Recalling Facts

1. Joe is
   - ❏ a. homesick.
   - ❏ b. happy.
   - ❏ c. physically ill.

2. Tom says that they might find
   - ❏ a. a new way home.
   - ❏ b. a treasure chest.
   - ❏ c. an apple orchard.

3. Joe says that he doesn't care for
   - ❏ a. hunting.
   - ❏ b. jumping.
   - ❏ c. swimming.

4. Tom calls Joe
   - ❏ a. a brave pirate.
   - ❏ b. a crybaby.
   - ❏ c. his best friend.

5. Joe says he wants to see his
   - ❏ a. brothers.
   - ❏ b. father.
   - ❏ c. mother.

## Understanding the Passage

6. Apparently, Joe, Huck, and Tom
   - ❏ a. have run away from home.
   - ❏ b. are on a school trip.
   - ❏ c. are playing in Tom's backyard.

7. The boy who wants to stay on the island the most is
   - ❏ a. Joe.
   - ❏ b. Tom.
   - ❏ c. Huck.

8. The most depressed boy is
   - ❏ a. Tom.
   - ❏ b. Joe.
   - ❏ c. Huck.

9. Joe doesn't want to
   - ❏ a. stay at the new swimming place.
   - ❏ b. pretend to be a pirate anymore.
   - ❏ c. both a and b.

10. Tom has no
    - ❏ a. mother.
    - ❏ b. sense of adventure.
    - ❏ c. imagination.

## 16 B *from* **The Beach of Falesá**
### *by Robert Louis Stevenson*

I saw that island first when it was neither night nor morning. The moon was to the west, setting, but still broad and bright. To the east, and right amidships of the dawn, which was all pink, the day-star sparkled like a diamond. The land-breeze blew in our faces, and smelt strong of wild lime and vanilla; other things besides, but these were the most plain; and the chill of it set me sneezing. I should say I had been for years on a low island near the line, living for the most part solitary among natives. Here was a fresh experience; even the tongue would be quite strange to me; and the look of these woods and mountains, and the rare smell of them, renewed my blood.

The captain blew out the binnacle-lamp.

"There!" said he. "There goes a bit of smoke, Mr. Wiltshire, behind the break in the roof. That's Falesá, where your station is, the last village to the east. Nobody lives to the windward. I don't know why. Take my glass, and you can make the houses out."

I took the glass; and the shores leaped nearer, and I saw the tangle of the woods and the breach of the surf, and the brown roofs and the black insides of houses peeped among the trees.

## 1. Recognizing Words in Context

Find the word *solitary* in the passage. One definition below is closest to the meaning of that word. One definition has the opposite or nearly the opposite meaning. The remaining definition has a completely different meaning. Label each definition C for *closest*, O for *opposite or nearly opposite*, or D for *different*.

_____ a. alone

_____ b. hidden

_____ c. together

## 2. Keeping Events in Order

Number each statement below 1, 2, or 3 to show the order in which the events took place.

_____ a. The narrator lives on a low island among natives.

_____ b. The narrator takes the captain's glass.

_____ c. The narrator sees Falesá's woods.

3. **Making Evaluations**

Two of the statements below describe things that actually happen or are stated in the passage. The other statement is an evaluation, or a judgment or opinion, about a character, setting, or event in the passage. Label each statement E for *evaluation* or H for *happens or is stated in the passage*.

_____ a. The narrator's station is in the last village to the east.

_____ b. The narrator is an adventurous man.

_____ c. The narrator has a fresh experience.

4. **Making Correct Inferences**

Two of the statements below are correct inferences, or reasonable guesses. They are based on information in the passage. The other statement is an incorrect, or faulty, inference. Label each statement C for *correct* inference or F for *faulty* inference.

_____ a. The narrator was lonely on his first island.

_____ b. The narrator enjoys experiencing new places and cultures.

_____ c. The narrator is not the first foreigner to land on this island.

5. **Summarizing**

One of the statements below is a summary that tells the most important ideas in the passage. The other two statements contain details from the passage. They do not tell the most important ideas in the passage. Label each statement S for *summary* or D for *details*.

_____ a. The moon is setting in the west and the sky is becoming pink.

_____ b. The narrator gets his first look at his new station on Falesá.

_____ c. The captain allows the narrator to look through his glass.

Correct Answers, Part A _____

Correct Answers, Part B _____

Total Correct Answers _____

# *from* Going A-Traveling
## *by The Brothers Grimm*

There was once a poor woman who had a son who wished to travel, but his mother said, "How can you travel? We have no money for you to take with you." Then said the son, "I will manage very well for myself. I will always say, 'Not much, not much, not much.'"

So he walked for a long time and always said, "Not much, not much, not much." Then he passed by a company of fishermen and said, "God speed you! Not much, not much, not much." "Miser, how dare you say, 'Not much'?" And when the net was drawn out they had not caught much fish. So one of them fell on the youth with a stick and said, "Have you never seen me threshing?" "What ought I to say, then?" asked the youth. "You must say, 'Get it full, get it full.'" After this he again walked a long time, and said, "Get it full, get it full," until he came to the gallows, where they had got a poor sinner whom they were about to hang. Then said he, "Good morning; get it full, get it full." "How dare you say, 'Get it full'? Do you want to make out that there are still more wicked people in the world—is not this enough?" And he again got some blows on his back. "What am I to say, then?" said he. "You must say, 'May God have pity on the poor soul.'"

Again the youth walked on for a long time and said, "May God have pity on the poor soul." Then he came to a pit by which stood a knacker who was cutting up a horse. The youth said, "Good morning; God have pity on the poor soul." "How dare you say that, you ill-tempered knave?" and the knacker gave him a box on the ear. "What am I to say, then?" "You must say, 'There lies the flesh in the pit!'"

So he walked on, and always said, "There lies the flesh in the pit; there lies the flesh in the pit." Then he came to a cart full of people. He said, "Good morning; there lies the flesh in the pit." The cart pushed him into a hole and the driver took his whip and cracked it upon the youth, till he was forced to crawl back to his mother.

**Reading Time** _____

## Recalling Facts

1. The woman and her son have no
   - ❏ a. home.
   - ❏ b. food.
   - ❏ c. money.

2. The son tells his mother he will always say,
   - ❏ a. "Not much, not much, not much."
   - ❏ b. "Too much, too much, too much."
   - ❏ c. "So much, so much, so much."

3. The son is called a miser by
   - ❏ a. the fishermen.
   - ❏ b. the farmers.
   - ❏ c. an old woman.

4. The son is taught to say, "There lies the flesh in the pit!" by the
   - ❏ a. poor sinner.
   - ❏ b. knacker.
   - ❏ c. hangman.

5. The knacker is cutting up a
   - ❏ a. cow.
   - ❏ b. horse.
   - ❏ c. pig.

## Understanding the Passage

6. The mother does not want her son to
   - ❏ a. make money.
   - ❏ b. travel.
   - ❏ c. go to school.

7. The son thinks the secret to success is
   - ❏ a. having money.
   - ❏ b. getting a job.
   - ❏ c. saying the right words.

8. Every time the son says something, he
   - ❏ a. gains friends.
   - ❏ b. upsets people.
   - ❏ c. improves his condition.

9. The "poor soul" the son sees at the gallows is the
   - ❏ a. fisherman.
   - ❏ b. sinner.
   - ❏ c. knacker.

10. After meeting a cart full of people, the son
    - ❏ a. finally learns to say the right thing.
    - ❏ b. decides he's had enough trouble and goes home.
    - ❏ c. goes straight to the gallows for his punishment.

# *from* **The Jungle Book**
## *by Rudyard Kipling*

Rikki-tikki was a mongoose, rather like a little cat in his fur and his tail but quite like a weasel in his head and his habits. His eyes and the end of his restless nose were pink. He could scratch himself anywhere he pleased, with any leg, front or back, that he chose to use. He could fluff up his tail till it looked like a bottlebrush, and his war cry, as he ran through the long grass, was: "*Rikk-tikk-tikki-tikki-tchk!*"

One day, a high summer flood washed him out of the burrow where he lived with his father and mother. It carried him, kicking and clucking, down a roadside ditch. He found a little wisp of grass floating there, and clung to it till he lost his senses. When he revived, he was lying in the hot sun on the middle of a garden path, very draggled indeed. A small boy was saying: "Here's a dead mongoose. Let's have a funeral."

"No," said his mother. "Let's take him in and dry him. Perhaps he isn't really dead."

They took him into the house. There a big man picked him up and said he was not dead but half choked. They wrapped him in cotton wool, and warmed him, and he opened his eyes and sneezed.

1. **Recognizing Words in Context**

   Find the word *draggled* in the passage. One definition below is closest to the meaning of that word. One definition has the opposite or nearly the opposite meaning. The remaining definition has a completely different meaning. Label each definition C for *closest*, O for *opposite or nearly opposite*, or D for *different*.

   _____ a. lively

   _____ b. dry

   _____ c. muddy

2. **Keeping Events in Order**

   Number each statement below 1, 2, or 3 to show the order in which the events took place.

   _____ a. The boy suggests having a funeral for Rikki-tikki.

   _____ b. The family wraps Rikki-tikki in cotton wool.

   _____ c. A flood washes Rikki-tikki out of his burrow.

## 3. Making Evaluations

Two of the statements below describe things that actually happen or are stated in the passage. The other statement is an evaluation, or a judgment or opinion, about a character, setting, or event in the passage. Label each statement E for *evaluation* or H for *happens or is stated in the passage*.

_____ a. A flood carries Rikki-tikki away from his parents.

_____ b. Rikki-tikki's habits are similar to a weasel's habits.

_____ c. The family that finds Rikki-tikki is caring and kind.

## 4. Making Correct Inferences

Two of the statements below are correct inferences, or reasonable guesses. They are based on information in the passage. The other statement is an incorrect, or faulty, inference. Label each statement C for *correct* inference or F for *faulty* inference.

_____ a. Rikki-tikki might have died without the family's help.

_____ b. Rikki-tikki is grateful for the chance to escape his parents.

_____ c. Rikki-tikki is usually full of energy.

## 5. Summarizing

One of the statements below is a summary that tells the most important ideas in the passage. The other two statements contain details from the passage. They do not tell the most important ideas in the passage. Label each statement S for *summary* or D for *details*.

_____ a. A family cares for Rikki-tikki after a flood sweeps him from his burrow.

_____ b. Rikki-tikki finds a wisp of grass in the roadside ditch and clings to it.

_____ c. A big man picks up Rikki-tikki and says that he is not dead but half choked.

Correct Answers, Part A _____

Correct Answers, Part B _____

Total Correct Answers _____

*from* **Sons and Lovers**

*by D. H. Lawrence*

Everybody was mad with excitement. William was coming on Christmas Eve. Mrs. Morel surveyed her pantry. There was a big plum cake, and a rice cake, jam tarts, lemon tarts, and mince pies. She was finishing cooking—Spanish tarts and cheesecakes. Everywhere was decorated. The kissing bunch of berried holly, hung with bright and glittering things, spun slowly over Mrs. Morel's head as she trimmed her little tarts in the kitchen. A great fire roared. There was a scent of cooked pastry. He was due at seven o'clock, but he would be late. The three children had gone to meet him. She was alone. But at a quarter to seven Morel came in again. Neither wife nor husband spoke. He sat in his armchair, quite awkward with excitement, and she quietly went on with her baking. Only by the careful way in which she did things could it be told how much moved she was. The clock ticked on.

"What time dost say he's coming?" Morel asked for the fifth time.

"The train gets in at half-past six," she replied.

"Then he'll be here at ten past seven."

"Eh, bless you, it'll be hours late on the Midland," she said indifferently. But she hoped, by expecting him late, to bring him early. Morel went down the entry to look for him. Then he came back.

"Goodness, man!" she said. "You're like an ill-sitting hen."

"Hadna you better be gettin' him summat t' eat ready?" asked the father.

"There's plenty of time," she answered.

"There's not so much as *I* can see on," he answered, turning crossly in his chair. She began to clear her table. The kettle was singing. They waited and waited.

Meantime the three children were on the platform at Sethley Bridge, on the Midland main line, two miles from home. They waited one hour. A train came—he was not there. Down the line the red and green lights shone. It was very dark and very cold.

"Ask him if the London train's come," said Paul to Annie, when they saw a man in a tip cap.

"I'm not," said Annie. "You be quiet—he might send us off."

But Paul was dying for the man to know they were expecting someone by the London train: it sounded so grand. Yet he was much too scared of broaching any man, let alone one in a peaked cap, to dare to ask.

**Reading Time** _____

## Recalling Facts

1. Mrs. Morel is finishing cooking
   - ❏ a. a big plum cake.
   - ❏ b. Spanish tarts.
   - ❏ c. a large turkey.

2. William is due
   - ❏ a. at seven o'clock.
   - ❏ b. at ten o'clock.
   - ❏ c. sometime the next day.

3. William is expected to arrive by
   - ❏ a. bus.
   - ❏ b. automobile.
   - ❏ c. train.

4. Mrs. Morel compares her husband to a
   - ❏ a. nervous hen.
   - ❏ b. half-baked duck.
   - ❏ c. big plum cake.

5. The three children wait on the platform at
   - ❏ a. Midland.
   - ❏ b. Sethley Bridge.
   - ❏ c. Charing Cross.

## Understanding the Passage

6. William has apparently been away for a
   - ❏ a. couple of days.
   - ❏ b. week.
   - ❏ c. long time.

7. Mrs. Morel has apparently spent the whole day
   - ❏ a. cooking.
   - ❏ b. sewing.
   - ❏ c. running errands.

8. Mrs. Morel and her husband
   - ❏ a. are deeply in love.
   - ❏ b. have little to say to each other.
   - ❏ c. keep interrupting each other.

9. Mr. Morel thinks William will be
   - ❏ a. home at any minute.
   - ❏ b. hours late.
   - ❏ c. arriving in the morning.

10. The Morels rarely
    - ❏ a. have visitors from London.
    - ❏ b. spend time in the kitchen.
    - ❏ c. light a fire in the fireplace.

## 18   B   *from* **The Octopus**
### *by Frank Norris*

The forward door of the railroad car opened and closed, and the school-teachers shrieked and cowered. The drummer with the revolver faced about, his eyes bulging. However, it was only the train conductor, hatless, his lantern in his hand. He was soaked with rain. He appeared in the aisle.

"Is there a doctor in this car?" he asked. Promptly the passengers surrounded him, voluble with questions. But he was in a bad temper. "I don't know anything more than you," he shouted angrily. "It was a holdup. I guess you know that, don't you? Well, what more do you want to know? I ain't got time to fool around. They cut off our express car and have cracked it open, and they shot one of our train crew, that's all, and I want a doctor."

"Did they shoot him—kill him, do you mean?"

"Is he hurt bad?"

"Did the men get away?"

"Oh, shut up, will you all?" exclaimed the conductor. "What do I know? Is there a *doctor* in this car, that's what I want to know?" A well-dressed young man stepped forward. "I'm a doctor," he said.

1. **Recognizing Words in Context**

   Find the word *voluble* in the passage. One definition below is closest to the meaning of that word. One definition has the opposite or nearly the opposite meaning. The remaining definition has a completely different meaning. Label each definition C for *closest*, O for *opposite or nearly opposite*, or D *for different*.

   _____ a. truthful

   _____ b. overflowing

   _____ c. hesitant

2. **Keeping Events in Order**

   Number each statement below 1, 2, or 3 to show the order in which the events took place.

   _____ a. A man steps forward and says that he is a doctor.

   _____ b. One of the members of the train crew is shot.

   _____ c. The conductor enters the railroad car.

## 3. Making Evaluations

Two of the statements below describe things that actually happen or are stated in the passage. The other statement is an evaluation, or a judgment or opinion, about a character, setting, or event in the passage. Label each statement E for *evaluation* or H for *happens or is stated in the passage.*

_____ a. The people on the train are in a dangerous situation.

_____ b. The passengers have many questions for the conductor.

_____ c. The conductor is looking for a doctor.

## 4. Making Correct Inferences

Two of the statements below are correct inferences, or reasonable guesses. They are based on information in the passage. The other statement is an incorrect, or faulty, inference. Label each statement C for *correct* inference or F for *faulty* inference.

_____ a. The passengers are afraid for their lives.

_____ b. The conductor does not fully understand what has happened.

_____ c. The passengers blame the conductor for what has happened.

## 5. Summarizing

One of the statements below is a summary that tells the most important ideas in the passage. The other two statements contain details from the passage. They do not tell the most important ideas in the passage. Label each statement S for *summary* or D for *details.*

_____ a. The conductor enters a passenger car looking for a doctor.

_____ b. The passengers in the railroad car shriek and cower in fear.

_____ c. The people who held up the train shot a member of the crew.

Correct Answers, Part A _____

Correct Answers, Part B _____

Total Correct Answers _____

84

# *from* The Club of Queer Trades
## *by G. K. Chesterton*

"What do you think of your Drummond Keith now?" asked Rupert. "We followed him home, and the very same night he is in the thick of a fatal, or nearly fatal, brawl, in which he is the only man armed. Really, if this is being glaringly good, I must confess that the glare does not dazzle me."

Basil was quite unmoved. "I admit his moral goodness is of a casual kind. He is very fond of change and experiment. But all the points you so cleverly make against him are mere coincidence. It's true he didn't want to talk about his house business in front of us. No man would. It's true that he carries a sword stick. Any man might. It's true he drew it in the shock of a street fight. Any man would. But there's nothing really dubious in all this. There's nothing to confirm—"

As he spoke a knock came at the door. "If you please, Sir," said the landlady, with a worried air, "a policeman wants to see you."

"Show him in," said Basil, amid the blank silence.

The heavy, handsome constable who appeared at the door spoke almost as soon as he appeared there. "I think one of you gentlemen," he said, curtly, but respectfully, "was present at the affair in Copper Street last night, and drew my attention very strongly to a particular man."

Rupert half rose from his chair. But the constable went on calmly, referring to a paper.

"A young man with gray hair. Had light gray clothes, very good, but torn in the struggle. Gave his name as Drummond Keith."

"This is amusing," said Basil, laughing. "I was in the very act of clearing that poor man's name. What about him?"

"Well, sir," said the constable, "I took all the men's addresses and had them watched. It wasn't serious enough to do more than that. All the other addresses are all right. But this man Keith gave a false address. The place doesn't exist."

The breakfast table was nearly flung over as Rupert sprang up, slapping both his thighs. "Well, by all that's good," he cried. "This is a sign from heaven."

"It's certainly very strange," said Basil quietly. "It's odd the fellow should have given a false address, considering he was perfectly innocent in the—"

"Oh, you jolly old duffer," cried Rupert. "You think every one as good as yourself."

**Reading Time** _____

## Recalling Facts

1. The brawl was
   - ❏ a. very mild.
   - ❏ b. fairly serious.
   - ❏ c. nearly fatal.

2. Drummond Keith carries a
   - ❏ a. concealed gun.
   - ❏ b. sword stick.
   - ❏ c. long knife.

3. When the policeman knocks, the door is opened by
   - ❏ a. the landlady.
   - ❏ b. Rupert.
   - ❏ c. Basil.

4. Basil says he was in the act of trying to clear
   - ❏ a. Rupert's name.
   - ❏ b. Keith's name.
   - ❏ c. his own name.

5. Rupert calls the policeman's news a sign from
   - ❏ a. the devil.
   - ❏ b. heaven.
   - ❏ c. the stars.

## Understanding the Passage

6. Rupert and Basil disagree over whether
   - ❏ a. Keith is guilty.
   - ❏ b. there was a brawl.
   - ❏ c. Keith carries a weapon.

7. During the brawl,
   - ❏ a. Keith was arrested.
   - ❏ b. the men ran away.
   - ❏ c. someone was nearly killed.

8. According to Basil, Keith's actions were
   - ❏ a. entirely outrageous.
   - ❏ b. totally peaceful.
   - ❏ c. not that terrible.

9. Copper Street must be where
   - ❏ a. Basil lives.
   - ❏ b. the brawl took place.
   - ❏ c. the police station is located.

10. Keith
    - ❏ a. is capable of violence.
    - ❏ b. sometimes lies.
    - ❏ c. both a and b.

# 19　B　*from* **Liberty Hall**

*by Ring Lardner*

The Thayers had a very pretty home and the room assigned to us was close to perfection. There were comfortable twin beds with a small stand and a convenient reading lamp between. If only we could have spent all our time in that guest room, it would have been ideal. But presently we were summoned downstairs to luncheon. I had warned Mrs. Thayer in advance and Ben was served with coffee. He drinks it black.

"Don't you take cream, Mr. Drake?"

"No. Never."

"But that's because you don't get good cream in New York."

"No. It's because I don't like cream in coffee."

"You would like our cream. We have our own cows and the cream is so rich that it's almost like butter. Won't you try just a little?"

"No, thanks."

"But just a little, to see how rich it is." She poured a tablespoon of cream into his coffee cup and for a second I was afraid he was going to pick up the cup and throw it in her face. But he kept hold of himself, forced a smile and declined a second chop.

"You haven't tasted your coffee," said Mrs. Thayer.

"Yes, I have," lied Ben. "The cream is wonderful. I'm sorry it doesn't agree with me."

## 1. Recognizing Words in Context

Find the word *declined* in the passage. One definition below is closest to the meaning of that word. One definition has the opposite or nearly the opposite meaning. The remaining definition has a completely different meaning. Label each definition C for *closest*, O for *opposite or nearly opposite*, or D for *different*.

_____ a. refused

_____ b. revealed

_____ c. accepted

## 2. Keeping Events in Order

Number each statement below 1, 2, or 3 to show the order in which the events took place.

_____ a. Ben and the narrator are asked to go downstairs.

_____ b. Ben lies to Mrs. Thayer.

_____ c. Mrs. Thayer pours cream into Ben's coffee cup.

## 3. Making Evaluations

Two of the statements below describe things that actually happen or are stated in the passage. The other statement is an evaluation, or a judgment or opinion, about a character, setting, or event in the passage. Label each statement E for *evaluation* or H for *happens or is stated in the passage*.

_____ a. The room assigned to Ben and the narrator is almost perfect.

_____ b. Ben forces a smile after Mrs. Thayer pours him cream.

_____ c. Mrs. Thayer chooses to be stubborn and pushy with Ben.

## 4. Making Correct Inferences

Two of the statements below are correct inferences, or reasonable guesses. They are based on information in the passage. The other statement is an incorrect, or faulty, inference. Label each statement C for *correct* inference or F for *faulty* inference.

_____ a. The narrator is familiar with Ben's habits.

_____ b. The Thayers are very open-minded people.

_____ c. Mrs. Thayer is proud of the cream that her cows produce.

## 5. Summarizing

One of the statements below is a summary that tells the most important ideas in the passage. The other two statements contain details from the passage. They do not tell the most important ideas in the passage. Label each statement S for *summary* or D for *details*.

_____ a. Mrs. Thayer tells Ben that the Thayers have their own cows and very good cream.

_____ b. The guest room contains comfortable twin beds and a convenient reading lamp.

_____ c. Ben does not want cream in his coffee, but Mrs. Thayer pours him cream anyway.

Correct Answers, Part A _____

Correct Answers, Part B _____

Total Correct Answers _____

A girl entered. She had a pale face, and very large black eyes that seemed to blaze at Nevada.

She came slowly toward him, with a movement he remembered even better than her tragic face. Life had evidently been harsher than ever to Lize Teller.

Nevada rose and shook hands with her.

"Jim Lacy!" she said, with stress of feeling that seemed neither regret nor gladness.

"Howdy, Lize!" drawled Nevada. "Reckon you're sort of surprised to see me heah."

"Surprised? Yes. I thought you had more sense," she returned.

"Wal now, Lize, that's not kind of you," he said, somewhat taken aback. "An I reckon I just don't get your hunch."

"Sit down, Jim," she rejoined, and as he complied she seated herself on the arm of his chair and leaned close. "I've been looking for you all afternoon. Lorenzo saw you ride in and stop at Mrs. Woods'."

"Ahuh! Wal, no wonder you wasn't surprised."

"But I am, Jim. Surprised at your nerve and more surprised at the look of you. What's happened? You've improved so I don't know you."

She leaned against him in a flirting way that Nevada had once found pleasing, though he had never encouraged it.

"Thanks, Lize. Wal, there was shore room for improvement. Nothin' much happened, except I've been workin' an' I quit the bottle."

"That's a lot, Jim, and I'm downright glad. I'll fall in love with you all over again."

"Please don't, Lize," he laughed. "I've quit throwin' guns, too. An' I reckon it'd be unhealthy for me, if you did."

"Probably will be, boy. You sure have me guessing," she replied, and she smoothed his hair and his scarf, while she gazed at him with deep, burning inquisitive eyes. "But don't try to lie to me about your gun tricks, sonny. You forget I'm the only one around Lineville who had you figured."

"Lize, I don't know as I remember that," he said, dubiously. He found she embarrassed him less than in former times. He had always feared Lize's overtures. But that dread was gone.

"Jim, you forget easily," she rejoined, with a touch of bitterness. "But God knows there was no reason for you to remember me. It was natural for me to miss you. For you were the only decent man I knew. But you treated me like you were a brother. That made me hate you."

**Reading Time** _____

## Recalling Facts

1. Nevada best remembers Lize's
   - ❏ a. tragic face.
   - ❏ b. movement.
   - ❏ c. little eyes.

2. Nevada greets Lize by
   - ❏ a. shaking hands.
   - ❏ b. kissing her.
   - ❏ c. bowing slightly.

3. Jim Lacy is also known as
   - ❏ a. Mr. Woods.
   - ❏ b. Nevada.
   - ❏ c. Lorenzo.

4. Lize is surprised at Jim's
   - ❏ a. nerve.
   - ❏ b. voice.
   - ❏ c. good sense.

5. Nevada has always feared Lize's
   - ❏ a. harshness.
   - ❏ b. overtures.
   - ❏ c. temper.

## Understanding the Passage

6. Lize has
   - ❏ a. lived a hard life.
   - ❏ b. inherited lots of money.
   - ❏ c. waited patiently for Nevada's return.

7. Lize thinks Nevada looks
   - ❏ a. better than ever.
   - ❏ b. worse than ever.
   - ❏ c. the same as ever.

8. Lize and Nevada have
   - ❏ a. just met.
   - ❏ b. never liked each other.
   - ❏ c. known each other for a long time.

9. Lize has
   - ❏ a. loved Nevada in the past.
   - ❏ b. never been in love.
   - ❏ c. tried to forget Nevada.

10. Nevada has
    - ❏ a. lived in Lineville all his life.
    - ❏ b. just returned to Lineville after being away.
    - ❏ c. never been to Lineville.

## 20 | B | *from* **The Awakening**
### *by Kate Chopin*

"What are you doing out here, Edna? I thought I should find you in bed," said her husband, when he discovered her lying in the hammock on the porch. He was returning home after walking Madame Lebrun back to her house. His wife did not reply.

"Are you asleep?" he asked, bending down close to look at her.

"No." Her eyes gleamed bright and intense, with no sleepy shadows, as they looked into his.

"Do you know it is past one o'clock? Come on," and he mounted the steps and went into their room.

"Edna!" called Mr. Pontellier from within, after a few moments had gone by.

"Don't wait for me," she answered. He thrust his head through the door.

"You will take cold out there," he said, irritably. "What folly is this? Why don't you come in?"

"It isn't cold; I have my shawl."

"The mosquitoes will devour you."

"There are no mosquitoes."

She heard him moving about the room, every second indicating impatience and irritation. Another time she would have gone in at his request. She would, through habit, have yielded to his desire; not with any sense of submission or obedience to his wishes, but unthinkingly, as we walk, move, sit, stand, go through the daily treadmill of the life which has been portioned out to us.

1. **Recognizing Words in Context**

   Find the word *yielded* in the passage. One definition below is closest to the meaning of that word. One definition has the opposite or nearly the opposite meaning. The remaining definition has a completely different meaning. Label each definition C for *closest*, O for *opposite or nearly opposite*, or D for *different*.

   _____ a. learned

   _____ b. gave in

   _____ c. rebelled

2. **Keeping Events in Order**

   Number each statement below 1, 2, or 3 to show the order in which the events took place.

   _____ a. Edna hears Mr. Pontellier moving about in their room.

   _____ b. Mr. Pontellier finds his wife lying in a hammock.

   _____ c. Mr. Pontellier walks Madame Lebrun back to her house.

## 3. Making Evaluations

Two of the statements below describe things that actually happen or are stated in the passage. The other statement is an evaluation, or a judgment or opinion, about a character, setting, or event in the passage. Label each statement E for *evaluation* or H for *happens or is stated in the passage*.

_____ a. Mr. Pontellier is irritated by his wife's refusal to come inside.

_____ b. Mr. Pontellier shows little respect for his wife.

_____ c. Edna's habit is to do whatever her husband wants her to do.

## 4. Making Correct Inferences

Two of the statements below are correct inferences, or reasonable guesses. They are based on information in the passage. The other statement is an incorrect, or faulty, inference. Label each statement C for *correct* inference or F for *faulty* inference.

_____ a. Mr. Pontellier does not understand his wife's behavior.

_____ b. Edna is tired of always obeying her husband.

_____ c. Edna often stays outside while her husband goes to bed.

## 5. Summarizing

One of the statements below is a summary that tells the most important ideas in the passage. The other two statements contain details from the passage. They do not tell the most important ideas in the passage. Label each statement S for *summary* or D for *details*.

_____ a. Edna's eyes gleam bright and intense, with no sleepy shadows.

_____ b. Edna refuses to go inside despite the request of her husband.

_____ c. Mr. Pontellier tells his wife that the mosquitoes will devour her.

Correct Answers, Part A _____

Correct Answers, Part B _____

Total Correct Answers _____

*from* **His Last Bow**

*by Arthur Conan Doyle*

"You say that the man came ten days ago and paid you for a fortnight's board and lodging?" asked Sherlock Holmes.

"He asked my terms, sir," said Mrs. Warren. "I said fifty shillings a week. There is a small sitting room and bedroom, and all complete, at the top of the house."

"Well?"

"He said, 'I'll pay you five pounds a week if I can have it on my own terms.' I'm a poor woman, sir, and Mr. Warren earns little, and the money meant much to me. He took out a ten-pound note, and he held it out to me then and there. 'You can have the same every fortnight for a long time to come if you keep the terms,' he said. "If not, I'll have no more to do with you.'"

"What were the terms?"

"Well, sir, they were that he was to have a key of the house. That was all right. Lodgers often have them. Also, that he was to be left entirely to himself and never, upon any excuse, to be disturbed."

"Nothing wonderful in that, surely?"

"Not in reason, sir. But this is out of all reason. He has been there for ten days, and neither Mr. Warren, nor I, nor the girl has once set eyes upon him. We can hear that quick step of his pacing up and down, up and down, night, morning, and noon; but except on that first night he has never once gone out of the house."

"Oh, he went out the first night, did he?"

"Yes, sir, and returned very late—after we were all in bed. He told me after he had taken the rooms that he would do so and asked me not to bar the door. I heard him come up the stair after midnight."

"But his meals?"

"It was his particular direction that we should always, when he rang, leave his meal upon a chair, outside his door. Then he rings again when he has finished, and we take it down from the same chair. If he wants anything else he prints it on a slip of paper and leaves it."

"Prints it?"

"Yes, sir; prints it in pencil. Just the word, nothing more. Here's one I brought to show you—SOAP. Here's another—MATCH. This is one he left the first morning—DAILY GAZETTE. I leave that paper with his breakfast every morning."

**Reading Time** _____

## Recalling Facts

1. For board and lodging, Mrs. Warren charges fifty shillings per
   - ❑ a. day.
   - ❑ b. week.
   - ❑ c. month.

2. The lodger offered to pay ten pounds every
   - ❑ a. fortnight.
   - ❑ b. week.
   - ❑ c. month.

3. The lodger asked Mrs. Warren
   - ❑ a. to give him fresh towels every day.
   - ❑ b. to bring his meals into his room.
   - ❑ c. never to disturb him.

4. On the first night, the lodger left the house and returned
   - ❑ a. at ten o'clock.
   - ❑ b. after midnight.
   - ❑ c. late the next morning.

5. The lodger orders special things by
   - ❑ a. ringing his bell.
   - ❑ b. printing on a piece of paper.
   - ❑ c. calling on the phone.

## Understanding the Passage

6. The lodger appears to be very
   - ❑ a. friendly.
   - ❑ b. secretive.
   - ❑ c. angry.

7. Mr. Warren does not
   - ❑ a. like the lodger.
   - ❑ b. like Mr. Holmes.
   - ❑ c. have a high-paying job.

8. The lodger hopes to stay at Mrs. Warren's for a
   - ❑ a. long time.
   - ❑ b. fortnight.
   - ❑ c. week.

9. The lodger is extremely
   - ❑ a. clear and direct.
   - ❑ b. confused and upset.
   - ❑ c. polite and reserved.

10. While in his room, the lodger does a lot of
    - ❑ a. reading.
    - ❑ b. sleeping.
    - ❑ c. walking.

## 21 B    *from* **The Mysterious Island**
### *by Jules Verne*

Two more hours passed and the balloon was scarcely 400 feet above the water.

At that moment a loud voice, the voice of a man whose heart did not know fear, was heard. To this voice responded others not less determined. "Is everything thrown out?" "No, here are still 2,000 dollars in gold." A heavy bag immediately plunged into the sea. "Does the balloon rise?" "A little, but it will not be long before it falls again." "What still remains to be thrown out?" "Nothing." "Yes! the car!" "Let us catch hold of the net, and into the sea with the car."

This was, in fact, the last hope of lightening the balloon. The ropes which held the car were cut. The balloon mounted 2,000 feet.

The five voyagers had hoisted themselves into the net. There they clung to the meshes, gazing downward.

The men had done all that men could do. No human efforts could save them now. They must trust to the mercy of He who rules the elements.

At four o'clock the balloon was only 500 feet above the surface of the water.

1.  **Recognizing Words in Context**

    Find the word *hoisted* in the passage. One definition below is closest to the meaning of that word. One definition has the opposite or nearly the opposite meaning. The remaining definition has a completely different meaning. Label each definition C for *closest*, O for *opposite or nearly opposite*, or D for *different*.

    _____ a. lifted

    _____ b. fastened

    _____ c. dropped

2.  **Keeping Events in Order**

    Number each statement below 1, 2, or 3 to show the order in which the events took place.

    _____ a. The men cut the ropes that hold the car.

    _____ b. The men throw 2,000 dollars in gold into the sea.

    _____ c. The balloon rises 2,000 feet.

3. **Making Evaluations**

Two of the statements below describe things that actually happen or are stated in the passage. The other statement is an evaluation, or a judgment or opinion, about a character, setting, or event in the passage. Label each statement E for *evaluation* or H for *happens or is stated in the passage*.

_____ a. Objects such as gold and cars are less important than people's lives.

_____ b. Cutting off the car is the last hope of lightening the balloon.

_____ c. The men have done all they can do.

4. **Making Correct Inferences**

Two of the statements below are correct inferences, or reasonable guesses. They are based on information in the passage. The other statement is an incorrect, or faulty, inference. Label each statement C for *correct* inference or F for *faulty* inference.

_____ a. The men had been planning to throw the money into the sea.

_____ b. The balloon is gradually sinking lower and lower.

_____ c. The less weight the balloon has to carry, the higher it can rise.

5. **Summarizing**

One of the statements below is a summary that tells the most important ideas in the passage. The other two statements contain details from the passage. They do not tell the most important ideas in the passage. Label each statement S for *summary* or D for *details*.

_____ a. The men rid their balloon of all objects in order to prevent it from sinking.

_____ b. The men respond to a man whose heart does not know fear.

_____ c. The five men pull themselves into the net and cling to the meshes.

Correct Answers, Part A _____

Correct Answers, Part B _____

Total Correct Answers _____

96

## *from* The House of Pride and Other Tales of Hawaii
### *by Jack London*

"Because we are sick they take away our liberty. We have obeyed the law. We have done no wrong. And yet they would put us in prison. Molokai is a prison. That you know. Niuli, there, his sister was sent to Molokai seven years ago. He has not seen her since. Nor will he ever see her. She must stay there until she dies. This is not her will. It is not Niuli's will. It is the will of the white men who rule the land. And who are these white men?

"We know. We have it from our fathers and our fathers' fathers. They came like lambs, speaking softly. Well might they speak softly, for we were many and strong, and all the islands were ours. As I say, they spoke softly. They were of two kinds. The one kind asked our permission, our gracious permission, to preach to us the word of God. The other kind asked our permission, our gracious permission, to trade with us. That was the beginning. Today all the islands are theirs, all the land, all the cattle—everything is theirs. They that preached the word of God and they that preached the word of Rum have foregathered and become great chiefs. They live like kings in houses of many rooms, with multitudes of servants to care for them. They who had nothing have everything, and if you, or I, or any Kanaka be hungry, they sneer and say, 'Well, why don't you work? There are the plantations.'"

Koolau paused. He raised one hand, and with gnarled and twisted fingers lifted up the blazing wreath of hibiscus that crowned his black hair. The moonlight bathed the scene in silver. It was a night of peace, though those who sat about him and listened had all the seeming of battle-wrecks. Their faces were leonine. Here a space yawned in a face where should have been a nose, and there an arm-stump showed where a hand had rotted off. They were men and women beyond the pale, the thirty of them, for upon them had been placed the mark of the beast.

They sat, flower-garlanded, in the perfumed, luminous night, and their lips made uncouth noises and their throats rasped approval of Koolau's speech. They were creatures who once had been men and women. But they were men and women no longer.

**Reading Time** _____

**Recalling Facts**

1. Koolau believes that Molokai is a
   ❏ a. resort.
   ❏ b. prison.
   ❏ c. big city.

2. Niuli's sister was
   ❏ a. sent to Molokai.
   ❏ b. married to a white man.
   ❏ c. in love with Koolau.

3. The people gathered around Koolau
   ❏ a. own the local plantations.
   ❏ b. wear garlands of flowers.
   ❏ c. want to move to Molokai.

4. This scene takes place in the
   ❏ a. morning.
   ❏ b. afternoon.
   ❏ c. evening.

5. Koolau's fingers are
   ❏ a. long and slender.
   ❏ b. twisted and gnarled.
   ❏ c. missing.

**Understanding the Passage**

6. Koolau is angry at
   ❏ a. Niuli.
   ❏ b. Niuli's sister.
   ❏ c. the white men.

7. When the white people came to the island, they
   ❏ a. became the slaves of the natives.
   ❏ b. took over everything.
   ❏ c. tried to make Koolau their leader.

8. Some of the people sitting around Koolau are
   ❏ a. disfigured.
   ❏ b. rich.
   ❏ c. blind.

9. The white traders gave the natives
   ❏ a. hibiscus.
   ❏ b. rum.
   ❏ c. weapons.

10. The people who now rule the island are the
    ❏ a. white men.
    ❏ b. Kanakas.
    ❏ c. sick people.

## 22  B   *from* **The Tree of Heaven**
### *by Robert W. Chambers*

Where was the canoe? There had always been one here—in his boyhood and ever since.

He dropped to his knees and parted the leafy thicket with his hands. There was no canoe there, nothing except a book lying on a luncheon basket.

He stared stupidly for a moment. Then he rose and stepped through the thicket to the edge of the water. A canoe glittered out there, pulled up on a flat sunny rock in midstream. On the rock lay a young woman in a dripping bathing dress drying her hair in the sun.

An odd sense of it all having happened before seized him. He recalled the sun on the water, the canoe, the slim figure lying there. And when she raised her hand, stifling a yawn, and stretched her arms, it seemed to him too familiar to surprise him.

Then, as she sat up, twisting her sun-bronzed hair, a chance turn of her head brought him into direct line of vision. They stared at one another across the water.

For one second the thought flashed on him that he knew her. Then in the same moment all that had seemed familiar in the situation faded into strangeness. He was aware that he had never seen her before.

1. **Recognizing Words in Context**

   Find the word *stifling* in the passage. One definition below is closest to the meaning of that word. One definition has the opposite or nearly the opposite meaning. The remaining definition has a completely different meaning. Label each definition C for *closest*, O for *opposite or nearly opposite*, or D for *different*.

   _____ a. enlarging

   _____ b. regarding

   _____ c. covering

2. **Keeping Events in Order**

   Number each statement below 1, 2, or 3 to show the order in which the events took place.

   _____ a. The man discovers that the canoe is not in the thicket.

   _____ b. The man and the woman stare at each other across the water.

   _____ c. The woman stifles a yawn and stretches her arms.

## 3. Making Evaluations

Two of the statements below describe things that actually happen or are stated in the passage. The other statement is an evaluation, or a judgment or opinion, about a character, setting, or event in the passage. Label each statement E for *evaluation* or H for *happens or is stated in the passage.*

_____ a. The man has an odd sense of it all having happened before.

_____ b. The woman is slim and has sun-bronzed hair.

_____ c. The man has difficulty understanding the situation.

## 4. Making Correct Inferences

Two of the statements below are correct inferences, or reasonable guesses. They are based on information in the passage. The other statement is an incorrect, or faulty, inference. Label each statement C for *correct* inference or F for *faulty* inference.

_____ a. The man does not know who the woman is.

_____ b. The man is upset that the woman has taken the canoe.

_____ c. The man had been planning to go out in the canoe.

## 5. Summarizing

One of the statements below is a summary that tells the most important ideas in the passage. The other two statements contain details from the passage. They do not tell the most important ideas in the passage. Label each statement S for *summary* or D for *details.*

_____ a. The man drops to his knees and finds a book lying on a luncheon basket in the thicket.

_____ b. After briefly thinking he knew the woman who took the canoe, the man realizes he's never seen her before.

_____ c. After pulling her canoe out of the lake, a young woman lies in the sun on a rock to dry her hair.

Correct Answers, Part A _____

Correct Answers, Part B _____

Total Correct Answers _____

# *from* The Elder-Tree Mother
## *by Hans Christian Andersen*

There was once a little boy who had caught cold. He had gone out and had somehow returned with wet feet. No one could imagine how it had happened, for it was quite dry weather. Now his mother undressed him, put him right to bed, and had the tea urn brought in to make him a good hot cup of elder tea, for that warms well. At the same time there also came in at the door the friendly old man who lived all alone at the top of the house. He had neither wife nor children, but he was very fond of little children, and knew so many stories that it was quite delightful.

"Now you are to drink your tea," said the mother. "Then perhaps you will hear a story."

"Ah! If one only could tell a new one!" said the old man, with a friendly nod. "But where did the little man get his wet feet?"

"That is a very good question," replied the mother. "No one can tell how that came about."

"Shall I have a story?" asked the boy.

"Yes, if you can tell me at all accurately—for I must know that first—how deep the gutter is in the little street through which you go to school."

"Just half way up to my knee," answered the boy. "That is, if I put my feet in the deep hole."

"You see, that's how we get our feet wet," said the old gentleman. "Now I ought certainly to tell you a story. But I don't know any more."

"You can make up one directly," answered the little boy. "Mother says that everything you look at can be turned into a story, and that you can make a tale of everything you touch."

"Yes, but those stories and tales are worth nothing! No, the real ones come of themselves. They knock at my forehead and say, 'Here I am!'"

"Will there soon be a knock?" asked the little boy, and the mother laughed out loud, and put elder tea in the pot, and poured hot water in it.

"A story! A story!"

"Yes, if a story would come of itself, but that kind of thing is very grand; it only comes when it's in the humor. Wait!" he cried all at once; "Here we have it. I can feel one starting to knock now!"

**Reading Time** _____

## Recalling Facts

1. The mother gives the boy a cup of
   - ❏ a. hot chocolate.
   - ❏ b. warm milk.
   - ❏ c. elder tea.

2. The friendly old man
   - ❏ a. is a stranger.
   - ❏ b. has no family of his own.
   - ❏ c. both a and b.

3. The old man is a great
   - ❏ a. storyteller.
   - ❏ b. grandfather.
   - ❏ c. hiker.

4. The old man finds out how the boy
   - ❏ a. got his feet wet.
   - ❏ b. liked being sick.
   - ❏ c. made up stories.

5. The old man wants to tell the boy a
   - ❏ a. new story.
   - ❏ b. ghost story.
   - ❏ c. sad story.

## Understanding the Passage

6. Among the children of the neighborhood, the old man is
   - ❏ a. something of a joke.
   - ❏ b. very popular.
   - ❏ c. a scary figure.

7. The boy does not
   - ❏ a. tell his mother how he got wet feet.
   - ❏ b. like the old man's stories.
   - ❏ c. both a and b.

8. After the boy tells him about the deep hole, the old man feels that the boy deserves to
   - ❏ a. get some rest.
   - ❏ b. hear a story.
   - ❏ c. have more tea.

9. The old man believes that his best stories come
   - ❏ a. from history books.
   - ❏ b. without his planning them.
   - ❏ c. after his daily cup of tea.

10. The mother believes that elder tea will
    - ❏ a. worsen her son's cold.
    - ❏ b. make her son feel better.
    - ❏ c. put the old man to sleep.

# *from* **Millie**

## *by Katherine Mansfield*

Millie sat quiet, thinking of nothing at all, her red swollen hands rolled in her apron, her feet stuck out in front of her, her little head with the thick screw of dark hair dropped on her chest. *Tick-tick* went the kitchen clock, the ashes clinked in the grate, and the venetian blind knocked against the kitchen window. Quite suddenly Millie felt frightened. A funny trembling started inside her—in her stomach—and then spread all over to her knees and hands. "There's somebody about." She tiptoed to the door and peered into the kitchen. Nobody there; the veranda doors were closed, the blinds were down, and in the dusky light the white face of the clock shone, and the furniture seemed to bulge and breathe . . . and listen, too. The clock—the ashes—and the venetian—and then again—something else, like steps in the backyard. "Go an' see what it is, Millie Evans."

She darted to the back door, opened it, and at the same moment someone ducked behind the woodpile. "Who's that?" she cried, in a loud, bold voice. "Come out o' that! I seen yer. I know where y'are. I got my gun. Come out from behind of that wood stack!"

1. **Recognizing Words in Context**

   Find the word *veranda* in the passage. One definition below is closest to the meaning of that word. One definition has the opposite or nearly the opposite meaning. The remaining definition has a completely different meaning. Label each definition C for *closest*, O for *opposite or nearly opposite*, or D for *different*.

   _____ a. closet

   _____ b. porch

   _____ c. car

2. **Keeping Events in Order**

   Number each statement below 1, 2, or 3 to show the order in which the events took place.

   _____ a. Millie sees someone duck behind the woodpile.

   _____ b. A funny trembling starts in Millie's stomach.

   _____ c. Millie tiptoes to the door and peers into the kitchen.

### 3. Making Evaluations

Two of the statements below describe things that actually happen or are stated in the passage. The other statement is an evaluation, or a judgment or opinion, about a character, setting, or event in the passage. Label each statement E for *evaluation* or H for *happens or is stated in the passage.*

_____ a. Millie acts bravely.

_____ b. Millie feels frightened.

_____ c. Millie cries out in a bold voice.

### 4. Making Correct Inferences

Two of the statements below are correct inferences, or reasonable guesses. They are based on information in the passage. The other statement is an incorrect, or faulty, inference. Label each statement C for *correct* inference or F for *faulty* inference.

_____ a. Millie is alone in the house.

_____ b. Millie is expecting a visitor.

_____ c. Millie has good intuition.

### 5. Summarizing

One of the statements below is a summary that tells the most important ideas in the passage. The other two statements contain details from the passage. They do not tell the most important ideas in the passage. Label each statement S for *summary* or D for *details.*

_____ a. Millie feels frightened and sees someone hide when she opens the back door.

_____ b. Millie sits with her hands rolled in her apron and her head on her chest.

_____ c. The veranda doors are closed, and the furniture seems to breathe.

Correct Answers, Part A _____

Correct Answers, Part B _____

Total Correct Answers _____

## *from* **The Eustace Diamonds**
### *by Anthony Trollope*

Lizzie, as she saw her aunt, made up her mind for the combat. "Oh, come ye in peace, or come ye in war?" she would have said had she dared. Her aunt had sent her love, but what of love could there be between those two? The Countess dashed at once to the matter in hand, making no allusion to Lizzie's ungrateful conduct to herself.

"Lizzie," she said, "I've been asked to come to you by Mr. Camperdown. I'll sit down, if you please."

"Oh, certainly, Aunt Penelope. Mr. Camperdown!"

"Yes, Mr. Camperdown. He has been to me because I am your nearest relation. So I am, and therefore I have come. I don't like it, I can tell you."

"Aunt Penelope, you've done it to please yourself," said Lizzie in a tone of insolence with which Lady Linlithgow had been very familiar with in former days.

"No, I haven't, miss. I have come for the credit of the family, if any good can be done toward saving it. You've got your husband's diamonds locked up somewhere, and you must give them back."

"My husband's diamonds were my diamonds," said Lizzie stoutly.

"They were family diamonds, Eustace diamonds, heirlooms—old property belonging to the Eustaces, just like their estates. Sir Florian didn't give 'em away, and couldn't, and wouldn't if he could. Such things ain't given away in that fashion. It's all nonsense, and you must give them up."

"Who says so?"

"I say so."

"That's nothing, Aunt Penelope."

"Nothing, is it? You'll see. Mr. Camperdown says so. All the world will say so. If you don't take care, you'll find yourself brought into a court of law, my dear, and a jury will say so. That's what it will come to. What good will they do you? You can't sell them; and, as a widow, you can't wear 'em. If you marry again, you wouldn't disgrace your husband by going about showing off the Eustace diamonds. But you don't know anything about 'proper feelings.'"

"I know every bit as much as you do, Aunt Penelope, and I don't want you to teach me."

"Then will you give up the jewels to Mr. Camperdown?"

"No, I won't."

"Or to the jewelers?"

"No, I won't. I mean to keep them for my child." Then there came forth a sob, and Lizzie's handkerchief was held to her eyes.

**Reading Time** _____

## Recalling Facts

1. Lizzie's conduct toward her aunt is
   - ❏ a. rude.
   - ❏ b. friendly.
   - ❏ c. warm and loving.

2. Mr. Camperdown comes to see Lizzie's aunt because
   - ❏ a. she is Lizzie's closest relative.
   - ❏ b. he wants to marry her.
   - ❏ c. they are old friends.

3. Lizzie's diamonds were given to her by her
   - ❏ a. father.
   - ❏ b. uncle.
   - ❏ c. husband.

4. Lizzie's aunt claims that the diamonds belong to
   - ❏ a. Lizzie.
   - ❏ b. herself.
   - ❏ c. the Eustace family.

5. Lizzie says she is keeping the diamonds for
   - ❏ a. her next husband.
   - ❏ b. herself.
   - ❏ c. her child.

## Understanding the Passage

6. Relations between Lizzie and her aunt are
   - ❏ a. cool but proper.
   - ❏ b. unfriendly.
   - ❏ c. affectionate.

7. Lizzie's aunt comes to see her
   - ❏ a. out of a sense of duty.
   - ❏ b. to renew an old friendship.
   - ❏ c. because she needs a loan.

8. Lizzie's aunt threatens her
   - ❏ a. with violence.
   - ❏ b. with legal action.
   - ❏ c. both a and b.

9. Lizzie's husband is
   - ❏ a. divorcing her.
   - ❏ b. in financial debt.
   - ❏ c. dead.

10. Lizzie's aunt suggests that Lizzie
    - ❏ a. can't really use the diamonds.
    - ❏ b. should sell the diamonds.
    - ❏ c. should give the diamonds to her child.

*from* **Les Miserables**
*by Victor Hugo*

The man took off his knapsack, placed it near the door, kept his stick in his hand, and sat down on a low stool near the fire. While going backward and forward the landlord still inspected his guest.

"Will supper be ready soon?" the man asked.

"Directly." While the newcomer had his back turned, the respectable landlord took a pencil from his pocket, and then tore off the corner of an old newspaper which lay on a small table. On the white margin he wrote a line or two, folded up the paper, and handed it to a lad who seemed to serve as page. The landlord whispered a word in the boy's ear, and he ran off in the direction of the Mayor's house. The traveler had seen nothing of all this, and he asked again whether supper would be ready soon. The boy came back with the paper in his hand, and the landlord eagerly unfolded it, like a man who is expecting an answer. He read it carefully, then shook his head, and remained thoughtful for a moment. At last he walked up to the traveler, who seemed plunged in anything but a pleasant reverie.

"I'm afraid I cannot make room for you, sir," he said.

1. **Recognizing Words in Context**

   Find the word *reverie* in the passage. One definition below is closest to the meaning of that word. One definition has the opposite or nearly the opposite meaning. The remaining definition has a completely different meaning. Label each definition C for *closest*, O for *opposite or nearly opposite*, or D for *different*.

   _____ a. song

   _____ b. discussion

   _____ c. daydream

2. **Keeping Events in Order**

   Number each statement below 1, 2, or 3 to show the order in which the events took place.

   _____ a. The traveler sits down on a stool near the fire.

   _____ b. The boy runs toward the Mayor's house.

   _____ c. The landlord tears off the corner of a newspaper.

### 3. Making Evaluations

Two of the statements below describe things that actually happen or are stated in the passage. The other statement is an evaluation, or a judgment or opinion, about a character, setting, or event in the passage. Label each statement E for *evaluation* or H for *happens or is stated in the passage.*

_____ a. The traveler seems to be having unpleasant thoughts.

_____ b. The landlord eagerly unfolds the piece of paper.

_____ c. The traveler is a suspicious man.

### 4. Making Correct Inferences

Two of the statements below are correct inferences, or reasonable guesses. They are based on information in the passage. The other statement is an incorrect, or faulty, inference. Label each statement C for *correct* inference or F for *faulty* inference.

_____ a. The traveler is a dangerous man.

_____ b. The landlord asked the Mayor about the traveler.

_____ c. The traveler is hungry.

### 5. Summarizing

One of the statements below is a summary that tells the most important ideas in the passage. The other two statements contain details from the passage. They do not tell the most important ideas in the passage. Label each statement S for *summary* or D for *details.*

_____ a. The traveler takes off his knapsack, sits down on a stool, and asks when supper will be ready.

_____ b. The landlord takes a pencil out of his pocket and rips off a piece of a newspaper.

_____ c. The landlord sends a note to the Mayor and then says he cannot feed the traveler.

Correct Answers, Part A _____

Correct Answers, Part B _____

Total Correct Answers _____

## 25    A     *from* Tom Sawyer, Detective

### *by Mark Twain*

"Quick, Huck, snatch on your clothes—I've got it! Bloodhound!"
In two minutes we was tearing up the river road in the dark towards the village. Old Jeff Hooker had a bloodhound, and Tom was going to borrow it. I says:

"The trail's too old, Tom—and besides, it's rained, you know."

"It don't make any difference, Huck. If the body's hid in the woods anywhere around the hound will find it. If he's been murdered and buried, they wouldn't bury him deep, it ain't likely, and if the dog goes over the spot he'll scent him, sure. Huck, we're going to be celebrated, sure as you're born!"

He was just a-blazing; and whenever he got afire he was most likely to get afire all over. That was the way this time. In two minutes he had got it all ciphered out, and wasn't only just going to find the corpse—no, he was going to get on the track of that murderer and hunt *him* down, too; and not only that, but he was going to stick to him till—

"Well," I says, "you better find the corpse first; I reckon that's a-plenty for today. For all we know, there *ain't* any corpse and nobody hain't been murdered. That cuss could 'a' gone off somers and not been killed at all."

That graveled him, and he says:

"Huck Finn, I never see such a person as you to want to spoil everything. As long as *you* can't see anything hopeful in a thing, you won't let anybody else. What good can it do you to throw cold water on that corpse and get up that selfish theory that there ain't been any murder? None in the world. I don't see how you can act so. I wouldn't treat you like that, and you know it. Here we've got a noble good opportunity to make a reputation, and—"

"Oh, go ahead," I says. "I'm sorry, and I take it all back. I didn't mean nothing. Fix it any way you want it. *He* ain't any consequence to me. If he's killed, I'm as glad of it as you are, and if he—"

"I never said anything about being glad; I only—"

"Well, then, I'm as *sorry* as you are. Any way you druther have it, that is the way *I* druther have it. He—"

"There ain't any druthers *about* it."

## Recalling Facts

1. Tom wants to borrow Jeff Hooker's
   - ❏ a. rifle.
   - ❏ b. map.
   - ❏ c. bloodhound.

2. Tom and Huck are looking for a
   - ❏ a. treasure.
   - ❏ b. dead body.
   - ❏ c. cave.

3. Tom is hoping to
   - ❏ a. become famous.
   - ❏ b. get a reward.
   - ❏ c. avoid trouble.

4. The boy more excited about the plan is
   - ❏ a. Tom.
   - ❏ b. Huck.
   - ❏ c. Jeff.

5. Huck isn't really sure there has been a
   - ❏ a. robbery.
   - ❏ b. fire.
   - ❏ c. murder.

## Understanding the Passage

6. Old Jeff Hooker lives in the
   - ❏ a. woods.
   - ❏ b. village.
   - ❏ c. city.

7. Tom is very
   - ❏ a. sure of himself.
   - ❏ b. uncertain.
   - ❏ c. frightened.

8. Tom is
   - ❏ a. working for the sheriff.
   - ❏ b. looking for adventure.
   - ❏ c. trying to help the accused murderer.

9. Tom gets upset with
   - ❏ a. Jeff.
   - ❏ b. his mother.
   - ❏ c. Huck.

10. Huck becomes very
    - ❏ a. apologetic.
    - ❏ b. angry.
    - ❏ c. shy.

## from **After Twenty Years**

*by O. Henry*

The policeman suddenly slowed his walk. In the doorway of a darkened hardware store a man leaned, with an unlighted cigar in his mouth. As the policeman walked up to him the man spoke up quickly.

"It's all right," he said. "I'm just waiting for a friend. It's an appointment made twenty years ago. Sounds a little funny to you, doesn't it? Well, I'll explain if you'd like to make certain it's all straight. About that long ago there used to be a restaurant where this store stands—'Big Joe' Brady's restaurant."

"Until five years ago," said the policeman. "It was torn down then."

"Twenty years ago tonight," said the man, "I dined here at 'Big Joe' Brady's with Jimmy Wells, my best chum, and the finest chap in the world. He and I were raised here in New York, just like two brothers. I was eighteen and Jimmy was twenty. The next morning I was to start for the West to make my fortune. You couldn't have dragged Jimmy out of New York. He thought it was the only place on earth. Well, we agreed that night that we would meet here again exactly twenty years from that date."

1. **Recognizing Words in Context**

   Find the word *straight* in the passage. One definition below is closest to the meaning of that word. One definition has the opposite or nearly the opposite meaning. The remaining definition has a completely different meaning. Label each definition C for *closest*, O for *opposite or nearly opposite*, or D for *different*.

   _____ a. improper

   _____ b. correct

   _____ c. whole

2. **Keeping Events in Order**

   Number each statement below 1, 2, or 3 to show the order in which the events took place.

   _____ a. The policeman walks up to the man in the doorway.

   _____ b. The man in the doorway agrees to meet his friend in twenty years.

   _____ c. "Big Joe" Brady's restaurant gets torn down.

## 3. Making Evaluations

Two of the statements below describe things that actually happen or are stated in the passage. The other statement is an evaluation, or a judgment or opinion, about a character, setting, or event in the passage. Label each statement E for *evaluation* or H for *happens or is stated in the passage*.

_____ a. The man in the doorway is a faithful friend.

_____ b. The man in the doorway explains why he is there.

_____ c. Jimmy liked New York.

## 4. Making Correct Inferences

Two of the statements below are correct inferences, or reasonable guesses. They are based on information in the passage. The other statement is an incorrect, or faulty, inference. Label each statement C for *correct* inference or F for *faulty* inference.

_____ a. The man in the doorway has not seen Jimmy for twenty years.

_____ b. At first the policeman is suspicious of the man in the doorway.

_____ c. Jimmy is no longer alive.

## 5. Summarizing

One of the statements below is a summary that tells the most important ideas in the passage. The other two statements contain details from the passage. They do not tell the most important ideas in the passage. Label each statement S for *summary* or D for *details*.

_____ a. The man in the doorway journeyed to the West to make his fortune.

_____ b. The policeman finds a man waiting for a friend he hasn't seen in 20 years.

_____ c. The policeman explains that the restaurant called "Big Joe" Brady's was torn down five years ago.

Correct Answers, Part A _____

Correct Answers, Part B _____

Total Correct Answers _____

112

# ANSWER KEY

# READING RATE GRAPH

# COMPREHENSION SCORE GRAPH

# COMPREHENSION SKILLS PROFILE GRAPH

# ANSWER KEY

| | | | | | | | | | |
|---|---|---|---|---|---|---|---|---|---|
| **A** | 1. b | 2. b | 3. b | 4. c | 5. c | 6. c | 7. a | 8. a | 9. b | 10. b |
| **B** | 1. O, C, D | 2. 1, 3, 2 | 3. H, H, E | 4. C, F, C | 5. D, D, S |
| **A** | 1. b | 2. c | 3. a | 4. b | 5. c | 6. a | 7. a | 8. c | 9. c | 10. b |
| **B** | 1. O, D, C | 2. 2, 1, 3 | 3. H, E, H | 4. C, C, F | 5. D, S, D |
| **3A** | 1. b | 2. c | 3. b | 4. b | 5. a | 6. c | 7. a | 8. c | 9. b | 10. a |
| **3B** | 1. C, O, D | 2. 1, 3, 2 | 3. E, H, H | 4. C, F, C | 5. S, D, D |
| **A** | 1. a | 2. b | 3. c | 4. a | 5. a | 6. b | 7. c | 8. b | 9. c | 10. b |
| **B** | 1. D, O, C | 2. 3, 1, 2 | 3. H, H, E | 4. F, C, C | 5. D, D, S |
| **5A** | 1. b | 2. a | 3. c | 4. c | 5. b | 6. a | 7. b | 8. b | 9. a | 10. b |
| **5B** | 1. O, C, D | 2. 3, 2, 1 | 3. H, E, H | 4. C, C, F | 5. S, D, D |
| **6A** | 1. b | 2. b | 3. b | 4. b | 5. a | 6. c | 7. a | 8. c | 9. b | 10. a |
| **6B** | 1. O, D, C | 2. 1, 2, 3 | 3. E, H, H | 4. C, F, C | 5. D, D, S |
| **7A** | 1. b | 2. c | 3. a | 4. a | 5. c | 6. c | 7. a | 8. a | 9. b | 10. b |
| **7B** | 1. O, C, D | 2. 2, 3, 1 | 3. E, H, H | 4. C, C, F | 5. D, S, D |
| **8A** | 1. c | 2. b | 3. a | 4. c | 5. a | 6. c | 7. a | 8. c | 9. a | 10. c |
| **8B** | 1. C, O, D | 2. 2, 3, 1 | 3. H, E, H | 4. C, F, C | 5. D, D, S |
| **9A** | 1. b | 2. c | 3. c | 4. a | 5. a | 6. a | 7. c | 8. b | 9. b | 10. b |
| **9B** | 1. O, D, C | 2. 3, 1, 2 | 3. E, H, H | 4. C, C, F | 5. S, D, D |
| **10A** | 1. a | 2. b | 3. b | 4. c | 5. c | 6. c | 7. a | 8. c | 9. a | 10. c |
| **10B** | 1. C, O, D | 2. 1, 3, 2 | 3. H, H, E | 4. F, C, C | 5. D, S, D |
| **11A** | 1. c | 2. a | 3. c | 4. a | 5. b | 6. b | 7. b | 8. a | 9. c | 10. b |
| **11B** | 1. D, O, C | 2. 3, 2, 1 | 3. H, H, E | 4. C, C, F | 5. S, D, D |
| **12A** | 1. b | 2. c | 3. b | 4. a | 5. a | 6. a | 7. b | 8. c | 9. a | 10. b |
| **12B** | 1. C, D, O | 2. 1, 3, 2 | 3. H, E, H | 4. F, C, C | 5. D, S, D |
| **A** | 1. c | 2. c | 3. b | 4. c | 5. a | 6. a | 7. c | 8. a | 9. b | 10. b |
| **B** | 1. O, C, D | 2. 2, 3, 1 | 3. H, H, E | 4. C, C, F | 5. D, D, S |

| | | | | | | |
|---|---|---|---|---|---|---|
| **14A** | 1. b  2. a | 3. b  4. c | 5. a  6. c | 7. b  8. a | 9. b  10. c | |
| **14B** | 1. C, D, O | 2. 1, 2, 3 | 3. H, E, H | 4. C, F, C | 5. D, S, D | |
| **15A** | 1. a  2.c | 3.b  4.b | 5. b  6. c | 7. a  8. a | 9. b  10. b | |
| **15B** | 1. D, O, C | 2. 2, 1, 3 | 3. E, H, H | 4. C, C, F | 5. D, D, S | |
| **16A** | 1. a  2. b | 3. c  4. b | 5. c  6. a | 7. b  8. b | 9. c  10. a | |
| **16B** | 1. C, D, O | 2. 1, 3, 2 | 3. H, E, H | 4. F, C, C | 5. D, S, D | |
| **17A** | 1. c  2. a | 3. a  4. b | 5. b  6. b | 7. c  8. b | 9. b  10. b | |
| **17B** | 1. D, O, C | 2. 2, 3, 1 | 3. H, H, E | 4. C, F, C | 5. S, D, D | |
| **18A** | 1. b  2. a | 3. c  4. a | 5. b  6. c | 7. a  8. b | 9. a  10. a | |
| **18B** | 1. D, C, O | 2. 3, 1, 2 | 3. E, H, H | 4. C, C, F | 5. S, D, D | |
| **19A** | 1. c  2.b | 3. a  4.b | 5. b  6. a | 7. c  8. c | 9. b  10. c | |
| **19B** | 1. C, D, O | 2. 1, 3, 2 | 3. H, H, E | 4. C, F, C | 5. D, D, S | |
| **20A** | 1. b  2. a | 3. b  4. a | 5. b  6. a | 7. a  8. c | 9. a  10. b | |
| **20B** | 1. D, C, O | 2. 3, 2, 1 | 3. H, E, H | 4. C, C, F | 5. D, S, D | |
| **21A** | 1. b  2. a | 3.c  4.b | 5. b  6. b | 7. c  8. a | 9. a  10. c | |
| **21B** | 1. C, D, O | 2. 2, 1, 3 | 3. E, H, H | 4. F, C, C | 5. S, D, D | |
| **22A** | 1. b  2. a | 3.b  4.c | 5. b  6. c | 7. b  8. a | 9. b  10. a | |
| **22B** | 1. O, D, C | 2. 1, 3, 2 | 3. H, H, E | 4. C, F, C | 5. D, S, D | |
| **23A** | 1. c  2. b | 3. a  4. a | 5. a  6. b | 7. a  8. b | 9. b  10. b | |
| **23B** | 1. O, C, D | 2. 3, 1, 2 | 3. E, H, H | 4. C, F,C | 5. S, D, D | |
| **24A** | 1. a  2.a | 3.c  4.c | 5. c  6. b | 7. a  8. b | 9. c  10. a | |
| **24B** | 1. D, O, C | 2. 1, 3, 2 | 3. H, H, E | 4. F, C, C | 5. D, D, S | |
| **25A** | 1. c  2. b | 3. a  4. a | 5. c  6. b | 7. a  8. b | 9. c  10. a | |
| **25B** | 1. O, C, D | 2. 3, 1, 2 | 3. E, H, H | 4. C, C, F | 5. D, S, D | |

# Reading Rate

Put an X on the line above each lesson number to show your reading time and words-per-minute rate for that lesson.

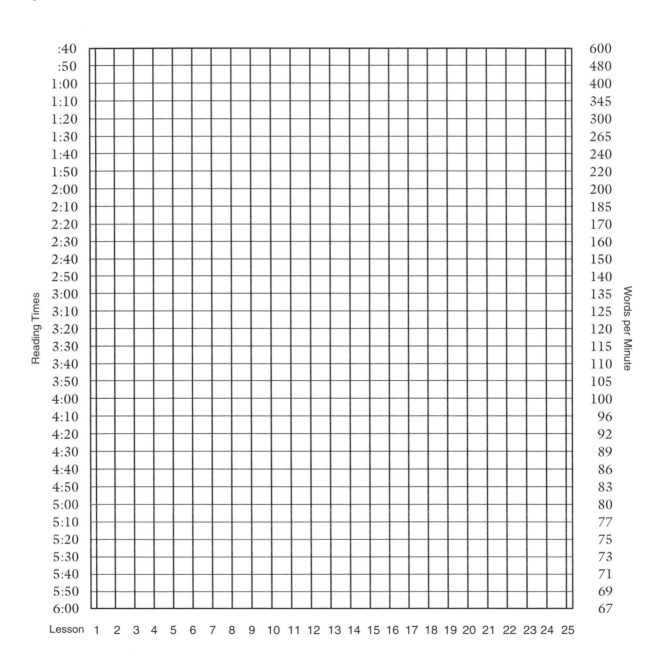

# COMPREHENSION SCORE

Put an X on the line above each lesson number to indicate your total correct answers and comprehension score for that lesson.

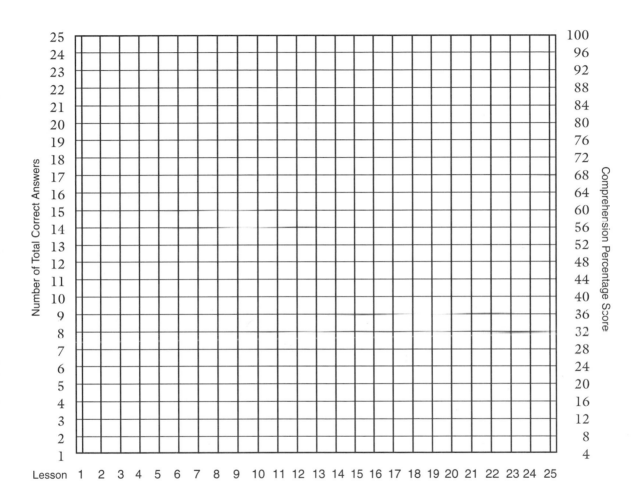

# COMPREHENSION SKILLS PROFILE

Put an X in the box above each question type to indicate an incorrect reponse to any question of that type.

| | Recognizing Words in Context | Keeping Events in Order | Making Evaluations | Making Correct Inferences | Summarizing |
|---|---|---|---|---|---|
| Lesson 1 | | | | | |
| 2 | | | | | |
| 3 | | | | | |
| 4 | | | | | |
| 5 | | | | | |
| 6 | | | | | |
| 7 | | | | | |
| 8 | | | | | |
| 9 | | | | | |
| 10 | | | | | |
| 11 | | | | | |
| 12 | | | | | |
| 13 | | | | | |
| 14 | | | | | |
| 15 | | | | | |
| 16 | | | | | |
| 17 | | | | | |
| 18 | | | | | |
| 19 | | | | | |
| 20 | | | | | |
| 21 | | | | | |
| 22 | | | | | |
| 23 | | | | | |
| 24 | | | | | |
| 25 | | | | | |